The Birds of Bidwell Park

Roger Lederer, PhD

Illustrated by
Carol Burr, PhD

THE BIRDS OF BIDWELL PARK

Copyright © 2010 by Roger Lederer

No part of this book may be reproduced in any form or by any means, electronic, mechanical, digital, photocopying or recording, except for the inclusion in a review, without permission in writing by the author: Roger Lederer, 4798 Songbird, Chico, CA 95973.

ISBN 978-0-615-36314-1

First Edition: April 2010

10 9 8 7 6 5 4 3 2 1

Printed in Bolivia — Industrias Gráficas Sirena

On the cover: Cedar Waxwing

This book is dedicated to Annie Bidwell who understood that open spaces are vital to the health of the community and the people who live there. As Chico has grown, these natural areas have provided important community spaces, habitat for plants and animals, recreational opportunities, places of natural beauty, and critical environmental areas like wetlands.

Annie's foresight has made Chico a special place that people have enjoyed for generations and that, we hope, future generations will also care for and appreciate. The birds are part of this precious legacy. Creating this book is our small way of thanking our founding mother and encouraging stewardship.

Table of Contents

Acknowledgements	i
Author and Artist Biographies	ii
Introduction	iii
How to Use this Book	v
Birdwatching	vi
The Parts of a Bird	vii
The Birds	1
Other Birds You Might See	79
Index	80
Bidwell Park Map	82
Notes	84

Acknowledgements

There are several people I have to thank for helping create The Bidwell Park Bird Book. Jackson Shedd, local artist, helped me formulate the idea for this book. My wife, the illustrator, saw this as an opportunity for us to work together on a professional project. Steve King, Scott Huber and his son Liam, avid birdwatchers and leading members of the local Altacal Audubon Society, reviewed the book and made very helpful suggestions. Dennis Beardsley kindly provided the map of Bidwell Park. Steve Baranoff gave permission to use his photo of the Cedar Waxwing for the basis of the illustration used on the cover and in the book. Ed McLaughlin provided input from the novice birdwatcher's point of view. Thanks also to Altacal Audubon and the Friends of Bidwell Park for their support of this project.

Olivia Calvin, creator of this Acorn Woodpecker and grandchild of the author and illustrator, was a major inspiration for this book. Without interest in and dedication to the protection of our natural resources by our and future generations, our lives and theirs will be diminished in countless tangible and intangible ways. We need to foster the interest of those coming after us through exposure to the beauty and importance of the natural world. Bidwell Park and thousands of other natural and nature-dominated sites need our protection. We are sure Annie Bidwell would have wished us to maintain this treasure which she donated to the City of Chico over a century ago. Watch birds with your children or grandchildren. You'll be giving them a lifetime ticket to the theater production that is nature.

There is nothing in which the birds differ more from man than the way in which they can build and yet leave a landscape as it was before.
- Robert Lynd

Author and Artist Biographies

Author

Dr. Roger Lederer is Professor Emeritus of Biological Sciences at California State University, Chico, whose interests are ecology, science education, and ornithology. He has a PhD from the University of Illinois, published over thirty scientific research papers, written a textbook entitled *Ecology and Field Biology*, and four previous books on birds: *Bird Finder*, *Pacific Coast Bird Finder*, *Amazing Birds*, and *Birds of New England*. Dr. Lederer has taught ornithology and ecology, consulted for governmental agencies, and volunteered for environmental organizations and schools. He has presented hundreds of public presentations to a wide variety of audiences, and through his website Ornithology.com been used as a resource by BBC, National Geographic, Weather Notebook, National Public Radio, National Canadian Television, Vanity Fair Magazine, *The Guinness Book of World Records*, The Weakest Link, Real Simple Magazine, the Detroit Free Press, Voice of America, and many other organizations and individuals. He was the first Endowed Professor of Environmental Literacy at CSU, Chico and served as Dean of the College of Natural Sciences for ten years. Dr. Lederer has traveled to and birdwatched in nearly 90 countries and served as lecturer on several cruise lines.

Illustrator

Dr. Carol Burr is Professor Emeritus of English at California State University, Chico, where she taught literature classes, created the Women's Studies and University Honors programs, served as Department Chair, and directed the Center for Multicultural and Gender Studies. With her students, she edited and published *Unstill Lives: Women of Northern California* and *Feeling for Place*. She drew the birds and symbols of this book using pen and colored pencils.

Introduction

Bidwell Park was deeded to the City of Chico by John and Annie Bidwell, the founders of Chico. The nearly 4,000-acre municipal park runs alongside Big Chico Creek Canyon for approximately eleven miles. From the campus of California State University, Chico, to the foothills of the Sierra Nevada, the park widens and encompasses trails, playgrounds, swimming holes, ball fields, golf and disc golf courses, paved and unpaved roads. The "Lower" Park west of Manzanita Avenue is partly wild but there is a lot of human activity; the "Upper" Park east of Manzanita Avenue has less human activity and more wild areas.

The noticeable difference between Upper and Lower Bidwell Park is terrain and habitat. Lower Park is fairly flat and level with a thick canopy of oak trees. Upper Park is mostly in the foothills of the Sierra Nevada Mountains with steep terrain and many rock formations. Upper Park widens on either side of Big Chico Creek and encompasses canyons and hills on either side as it moves into the foothills on a gravel road. As the park moves eastward, it becomes less of a forest and more of a savannah with Horseshoe Lake and the Bidwell Park Golf Course intervening.

Many cities point to their open spaces as very special, but Bidwell Park is really the jewel in the crown of Chico. A very distinctive place respected and revered by the citizens of Chico, all seem to think they know it well, but there is a lot more to the park than many people realize. Hikers and bikers know the trails, baseball and soccer participants are familiar with fields, summer users know all the picnic areas, and parents and grandparents know Caper Acres and other children's play areas. A much smaller proportion of park users recognize the flora and fauna — the trees, wildflowers, vines, and shrubs, some native and some not. Squirrels, deer, raccoons, opossums, lizards, snakes, newts, salamanders, and a variety of fish inhabit the park's boundaries, often unnoticed. People are more aware of birds because they are active, colorful, and talkative. But without effort on the part of the observer, all birds seem alike. This book is an attempt to give personalities to the varied but most common birds of Bidwell Park.

Although not a comprehensive field guide, you should be able to use this book to identify virtually all of the birds you are likely to spot in the park during a casual stroll or a long hike any time of year.

Bidwell Park is a wonderful place to see birds because it is both semi-wild and very accessible. It is good birdwatching for both the beginner and expert. Because of the terrain, vegetation, human use, and elevation change, the bird life is a bit different between the western and eastern parts of the park. Nearly 200 species of birds have been seen in Bidwell Park, but some are seen only at certain times of the year and others rarely at any time.

The Big Chico Creek Nature Center is the gateway to and the official information center for Bidwell Park. Up the canyon, Bidwell Park meets the Big Chico Creek Ecological Reserve where book is also appropriate. Enjoy.

How to Use this Book

The real goal of this book is to encourage the reader to develop an interest in and begin to notice the great variety of birds in Bidwell Park, which will enhance every park visit. We have tried to point out the most interesting aspects of each bird and provide a hint or two about how to identify it and where it will most likely be seen. Only adult male plumage is pictured although female and immature plumages may differ. There are 86 bird species described even though more than twice that many species might be seen in the park over a year of birdwatching. In this book are the birds you are most likely to see on a short walk through any part of the park. The sizes of the bird illustrations are not to scale but are relative to their actual sizes, as noted in the text.

Seasonal tree symbols indicate whether the species is likely to be seen during the spring, summer, fall, winter, or all year:

Spring   *Summer*   *Fall*   *Winter*

The book indicates whether each bird is most likely to be seen in lower park, upper park, or both. And the section of the park in which the bird is most likely to be seen is indicated by symbols:

Forest   *Savannah*   *Forest/Savannah*

Creek   *Pond*   *Grassland*   *Golf Course*

On each page, a sidebar offers an especially noteworthy fact about the bird.

If this book encourages you to pursue birdwatching more seriously, you might wish to purchase a detailed field guide to the birds of the western U.S. Meanwhile, enjoy *The Birds of Bidwell Park*.

Birdwatching

They say the best birdwatcher is another bird. What you look for may not be what another bird looks for. Strolling by yourself, you notice only the occasional jay or robin, but after you go on a casual jaunt with an avid birdwatcher, an entire new world opens to you. Jays, sparrows, warblers, woodpeckers, hawks, and vultures are now everywhere. They were always there but you focused on other things.

When you try to identify birds, you have to look at them in a new way. There is typically no one characteristic that distinguishes one bird from another; it's a set of characteristics. Just as there is not one way to tell a make and model of automobile from another, there is no single characteristic to tell birds apart. All autos have headlights, tires, bumpers, windshields, and other parts in common. All birds have feathers, beaks, scaled legs, tails, and wings. But the variation in those parts, plus the coloration and patterning of the feathers, makes each species unique and most are easy to identify.

Study the diagram on the following page and become familiar with the general parts of a bird. Besides the clues about size, shape, bill, pattern, habitat, behavior, and color, here are other helpful hints:

Obtain a decent pair of binoculars. The magnification, lens size, and features of a binocular are personal choice, but a 7x35 or 8x42 pair seems to be most birdwatchers' preference.

Always locate a bird with your naked eye first. Binoculars give you a narrow field of view and it is hard to find a bird by scanning with them. And scan from right to left; we read from left to right and scanning in the opposite direction slows down the scan.

Songs and Calls can be a very good clue or even THE clue to identifying a bird, but it takes some experience to learn these.

Finally, my best recommendation for the beginning birdwatcher: go out in the field with those folks who know the birds. If you don't have a friend who does, contact the local Altacal Audubon Society or Big Chico Creek Nature Center.

The Parts of a Bird

This is a diagram of a typical bird, showing the major body areas. The identification of a bird in the field is largely dependent upon a variety of characteristics called "field marks". These may be bill shape, plumage pattern, crest, length of legs, or anything else.

There is no one way to identify birds, but there are major clues. By following these clues, you can eliminate possibilities and narrow your choices. The clues are:

Size – sparrows and thrushes are distinctly smaller than hawks and bigger than kinglets, for example.

Shape – is it tall and thin or short and round? Does it have wide or narrow wings or tail? The silhouette of the bird can tell you a lot.

Bill – both size and shape are important. Is it long, hooked, upcurved, stout?

Pattern – does it have patches, stripes, splotches or bars on the background color, wing, or tail of the bird?

Habitat – is it in a marsh, a forest, grassland or lake?

Behavior – is it pecking on a tree, probing in the grass, swimming, or soaring?

Color – although looking for color seems obvious, color can be missing or misleading. The bird may be in dark shade, making it appear dark or even black or it might be in bright direct light, making colors look different than they would in a moderate light. But in good light, color is very helpful.

Using one or two of these clues is often sufficient to identify a bird, or at least put it into a smaller group, such as sparrow or swallow. It just takes a bit of practice.

The Birds

The Birds of Bidwell Park

Great Blue Heron
UPPER PARK

The Great Blue Heron is one of the more common wetland birds and the largest North American heron. About four feet tall with blue-gray plumage, a long neck, and shaggy feathers on the neck and back, it is often seen along roads and highways with its head motionless and crooked at a 45º angle ready to spear or snatch prey. The heron has a close and similar relative in Europe, the Great Gray Heron. Unlike distantly related cranes which fly with outstretched necks, herons and egrets fold their necks back on their shoulders while in flight. With a wingspread of six feet, upon liftoff these large and ungainly birds remind one of a prehistoric flying creature. The only time its harsh croaking voice is heard is upon their rising into the air, making their appearance a bit of a surprise.

Herons nests in large colonies on rough platforms of twigs, often on the ground among marsh reeds but also in trees with egrets. Herons feed as individuals on aquatic animals such as frogs, crayfish, and fish in streams and marshes, spearing them with sharp serrated bills. Herons will also eat voles and mice. The Great Blue Heron hunts by walking slowly and standing motionless in shallow water, waiting for an unwary fish to swim by. If the fish is large the heron will often take it to the shore to dismember it. Sometimes a heron actually chokes and dies from eating a fish that is too big for its throat.

Although Great Blue Herons inhabit fish hatcheries and are blamed for taking young fish, a recent study found that most of the fish that are taken were sick, stayed near the surface, and would have died anyway.

Look for the Great Blue Heron along the creek in the Upper Park and around the shores of Horseshoe Lake year round.

An adaptation of the sixth cervical vertebra allows the bird to curl its neck into an S-shape and thrust it forward with lightning speed to capture prey.

Green Heron
UPPER & LOWER PARK

The Green Heron, once called the green-backed heron, is a wading bird about the size of a crow, common in wetlands. It has a grayish green back and chestnut undersides broken by wide white streaks. Secretive, preferring to be active in the evening or early morning, it walks stooped and slowly while it stalks prey along a well vegetated river or stream, or the shores of a lake or pond, and is not easy to spot. You are most likely to see it when it bolts into the air, having been frightened by your approach. It will stand motionless, occasionally raising its dark green head crest, until it sees some aquatic creature such as small fish, crayfish, or frogs which it will rapidly snatch with a spear-like thrust of its bill. It will even drop bits of food items such as worms, berries, or small sticks on the surface of the water to attract fish; it is one of the few birds that uses tools!

There is no biological difference between herons and egrets; "heron" comes from the German and "egret" from the French. By custom, though, herons are dark and egrets are white.

Solitary most of the year, during the mating season the male calls to the female with a screeching squawk, an unmelodic sound typical of herons and egrets. Many other herons nest in colonies, but the Green Heron pair nests alone. The male gathers nesting materials of sticks and twigs while the female builds the nest. Both parents incubate the eggs until they hatch in three weeks. Both male and female feed the young by regurgitating partly digested food into the young birds' mouths when the young signal the parents to do so by pecking at their bill.

Green Herons are resident year round along Big Chico Creek, but those in the Pacific northwest migrate southward, so there are more in Bidwell Park in the winter than in the summer. The Green Heron has a variety of colloquial names across the county, including "whitepoke", "chalkline", "fly-up-the-creek" and "green bittern."

Canada Goose
UPPER PARK

Canada Geese vary from four to 20 pounds. The populations are variously called Dusky, Richardson's, Common, *etc.*, but they are all the same species of Canada Goose except for the smallest, which has been designated as a new species called the "Cackling Goose." "Canadian Geese" as they are often called, is a misnomer because many geese are Canadian. Hundreds of thousands of Canada Geese winter in the California Valley. But some populations are non-migratory and a few spend all year in Butte County and in Bidwell Park. You often see them at Horseshoe Lake. You may also see a number of unusual looking waterfowl at Horseshoe Lake because both ducks and geese interbreed with other wild species as well as domestic ones. Canada Geese will often mate with the domestic goose (actually a domestic breed of the Graylag Goose), with the offspring looking like a heavily bleached Canada Goose.

Overhunted and in serious decline a hundred years ago, Canada Geese have become the most common waterfowl species in North America and are considered pests in some areas, eating and defecating on lawns, school grounds, and golf courses and posing hazards at airports. Pretty casual about nesting sites in suburban areas, they may nest near homes, in parks, on the ground, on telephone poles, *etc.*, laying three to eight eggs per clutch. Canada Geese are monogamous and show long term pair bonding but they do "divorce" and if one dies, the other will find a new mate.

Like all waterfowl and a number of other birds, incubation is delayed until the last egg is laid; this insures that all young hatch at the same time; essential if young are to leave the nest immediately.

Canada Geese are known for their V-shaped formations in migratory flight. This configuration of flying birds has shown to be aerodynamically efficient for most birds in the flock. The lead bird works the hardest, getting no lift from the other birds, so it drops back and another takes over. There is no "leader" leading the flock.

Wood Duck
UPPER & LOWER PARK

The Wood Duck is certainly one of the world's most beautiful birds. With a variety of colors, patterns, iridescent feathers and a red eye, it is unmistakable. The much drabber brown female can be told by her white eye ring. Smaller than a Mallard, the Wood Duck is a perching duck which nests in trees. They can be seen near the Five-Mile pool and almost anywhere along the creek with minimal human activity.

An unusual practice by some hole nesting ducks is that of "nest dumping" where several females may lay eggs in the same nest; the nest box might eventually contain several dozen eggs or more, few of which hatch. Apparently this is the result of a lack of nesting sites.

Their typical nest sites are tree cavities, but artificial Wood Duck boxes have been put up in many private and public areas with great success. The nesting sites are typically over or near water and may be 20 to 100 feet above ground. The highest ever noted was 240 feet. There are no perches on the box and parents enter it by flying right to the opening, folding their wings, and entering. What makes this nesting habit most interesting is that the dozen or so young, the day after hatching, climb to the nest box opening and jump out, falling to the ground like lumps of feathered clay.

The Wood Duck feeds by dabbling in the water or feeding on land on berries, seeds, or invertebrates. Their call is a distinctive whistle.

Wood Ducks were in serious decline a century ago as they were hunted for food as well as the feather market for ladies' hat decorations. Today they are more common because their hunting is restricted and artificial nest boxes provided by conservation groups and agencies have made many more nesting sites available.

Mallard
UPPER & LOWER PARK

The Mallard, the most common duck in North America (perhaps ten million of them) and familiar to everyone, is the only duck that truly makes a "quacking" sound as the other species whistle, grunt, and make other noises the average person does not expect from a duck. The male's green head is set off by a grayish body while the female is mostly brownish. Both have an iridescent purple patch on their wings called a "speculum", which makes them identifiable in flight. They are omnivorous and will eat a large variety of foods, including corn, wheat, rice, willow, small clams and fish, insects, and even frogs. Because they don't dive but stick their heads under the water while their rear ends rise out of the water, they are called "dabbling ducks". Almost all the domestic duck varieties we are familiar with are derived from the Mallard and the name comes from the Old French word "malhard" which means "hardy or brave".

The alula is a small set of feathers extending from the thumb that allows the Mallard (and other birds) to take off at a very steep angle, as slats do on jet planes.

Although most ducks leave the California valley to fly north to their breeding grounds in Canada and elsewhere, many Mallards remain in the valley to raise their family, including a few in Bidwell Park along the slower areas of the creek such as the Five Mile recreation area and in Horseshoe Lake. Courtship and pairing up occurs in the fall and winter. In the spring, nine to 13 eggs are laid. After about a month, the ducklings hatch within 24 hours of each other and are led to the water by the female who looks over them. The male hangs out with other males, all of whom lose their courtship plumage, take on a female plumage (called "eclipse plumage"), and are flightless for a short time during the summer. In the fall the males renew their breeding plumage. Mallards are found most often in Horseshoe Lake and slower waters of Big Chico Creek. A variety of hybrids between Mallards and domestic ducks are frequently seen at Horseshoe Lake.

Turkey Vulture
UPPER & LOWER PARK

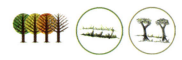

The Turkey Vulture may seem like an unappealing bird with a naked red head, hooked and ivory-colored bill, and the habit of eating dead creatures, but they are important in cleaning up the natural environment. They have an extremely well-developed sense of smell and are attracted by a chemical formed by the decaying process, but they also detect their decaying prey with their excellent eyesight. It is a rare occurrence, but Turkey Vultures will occasionally take live prey such as squirrels or even spraying skunks.

Riding updrafts of air from warm roadways and rooftops or wind currents deflected off of hills and mountains, Turkey Vultures can soar for hours on end, looking for food or each other. Suitable soaring conditions is what brings them together in circling flocks, not a dead animal (otherwise, they would land!). It is easy to tell these hawk-like birds from hawks and eagles because of their smaller heads (which lack feathers), and the way they hold their wings in a V with the tips upraised (a dihedral shape). Hawks do not usually raise their wingtips and eagles fly with their wings flattened. The front of vultures' wings are brownish and the rear a grayish-brown, giving them a two-toned appearance in the right light. On the ground they somewhat resemble turkeys, hence their name.

Turkey Vultures, after gorging themselves, might be so full that they cannot escape a predator. In case of a predator attack, they will vomit, hence their family name of Cathartidae, deriving from "catharsis", to throw up.

They are often seen in trees with wings outspread, drying their wings to rid themselves of parasites. They occasionally nest in trees but more often on the ground or in hollow logs or caves. They build a minimal nest, really just a depression in the ground, where one to three eggs are laid. You will not hear them as they lack the typical voice box of birds, but they can make a soft hiss or groan.

Recent DNA evidence indicates that vultures are more closely related to ibises and storks than they are to hawks and eagles.

White-tailed Kite
UPPER PARK

The White-tailed Kite, formerly called the Black-shouldered Kite, is often seen over grasslands, marshes, sparse woodlands and unplowed farm fields, and it is an unmistakable bird. A reddish eye contrasts with a white body with gray wings and black shoulders, and of course a white tail. Occasionally gulls and White-tailed Kites are confused because their shape and coloration are similar, but gulls do not have the black shoulder and have longer bills.

This raptor alternately hovers and then soars for short distances at a height of 10-40 feet over grasslands, searching for its prey of mice, voles, squirrels, snakes, insects, and most any other animal living amongst the grass, and when it detects it prey, the bird studies it for a second while hovering in place, facing the wind and scanning the ground. The kite then swoops in for the kill, wings in a nearly vertical position, dropping feet first, feeding much like the American Kestrel. Kites rarely eat birds.

Although some individuals wander long distances in search of food, most are non- migratory and may gather in large roosts of up to several dozen birds in the winter. Once shot in large numbers early in the 20th century by farmers who thought they were eating chickens, they were on the verge of extinction with only 70 pairs in existence in the 1930's and 40's. Egg collectors contributed to the decline in White-tailed Kite numbers as well. With protection by the State of California their numbers recovered but they are again threatened, this time due to loss of habitat, and their distribution in California is spotty, being found mostly in the Central Valley and southern coast. In Bidwell Park, the open grassland in Upper Park is their preferred hunting area. Look for them around the Easter cross.

Birds we call kites were not named after the toy we fly on a string, but the other way around. Originally the word "kite" came from the Old English "cyta" meaning to move swiftly, as these birds do when they attack prey.

Osprey
UPPER & LOWER PARK

The Osprey is a one-of-a-kind bird found all over the world except Antarctica. It eats fish exclusively and is elegantly designed to do so. A medium sized hawk, its black and white markings, crook in its elbow, and watery habitat easily identify this bird. It flies up and down creeks or searches over bodies of water for its likely prey. When it spots a fish, it folds its wings and dives to and sometimes into the water. With a mighty struggle, the bird lifts itself and the fish out of the water and flies off, with the prey aerodynamically held head first in the bird's talons. Its feet are well adapted for this lifestyle, with a reversible toe that can change the foot quickly from three toes forward and one back to an arrangement of two and two. Not only is this toe arrangement more effective in catching fish, but the talons are heavily curved and the underside of the toes have pointed, prickly scales with which to grasp the slimy prey. It is successful in catching a fish about 30 percent of the time.

The name "osprey" comes from the Greek and means "bone breaker". Rarely, it is called the Sea Hawk as it also fishes on ocean shores.

Ospreys require two perches for nesting, usually dead snags or power poles or one of each. The Osprey pair builds a nest which may be used year after year and get larger and larger and the male uses another perch as a "pilot perch" where he sits and guards the nest when not fishing for the young. When a fish is brought back to the nest, the head is usually eaten, but the rest of the body may not be.

Ospreys are migratory and will typically be seen in Bidwell park only during the spring and fall where they might been seen stopping for a snack at Horseshoe Lake or Big Chico Creek's wide swimming holes.

Cooper's/Sharp-shinned Hawks
UPPER & LOWER PARK

Sharp-shinned and Cooper's Hawks live in a wide variety of forest types throughout North America. They are permanent residents in Bidwell Park but their population increases when migrants arrive for the winter. They are very similar birds in shape, coloration, habitat and habits, but the pictured Cooper's Hawk is about 1/3 larger at 16 inches, the Sharp-shinned being about 11 inches but the females are similar in size to the male Coopers'. Both have a dark cap with a blue-gray back but the Cooper's has a larger head that sticks out farther in front of the wings than does the Sharp-shinned.

Birds constitute the vast majority of the hawks' diet, using their fast, agile flight to catch their prey. They may also take small mammals, frogs, lizards, and insects. They often make a living in the winter by hanging around bird feeders waiting for prey. One would think that putting up bird feeders might be leading finches and sparrows to an untimely demise, but studies have shown that without bird feeders more birds would die of starvation than are taken by hawks at feeders. In the 1960's and 70's Sharp-shinned Hawks declined in number due to DDT but have recovered nicely since its ban and the proliferation of bird feeders. Cooper's Hawks are more common in Bidwell Park since they are permanent residents while Sharp-shinned Hawks are winter visitors.

Both species capture prey by flying through dense vegetation cover and autopsies have shown that the hawks incur fractures to their shoulder bones as a result.

Being what are called "accipiters", both Cooper's and Sharp-shinned do not soar like "buteos" (Red-tailed and Red-shouldered Hawks, *e.g.*) but show a pattern of flapping and gliding, more of the former and less of the latter. The females of all hawks are about 1/3 larger than the male, but in the case of the Sharp-shinned Hawk, the female is almost twice the size of the male.

Red-shouldered Hawk

UPPER & LOWER PARK

The Red-shouldered Hawk should perhaps be called the "Red-bellied Hawk," as the Pacific race has undersides of a deep, bright rusty color. The red-shouldered name comes from the eastern U.S. populations that exhibit this color only on their "shoulders", which are actually their wrists. These medium-sized hawks prefer mixed deciduous and riparian forests but unlike other soaring hawks do not shy away from populated areas and can be found nesting in lower Bidwell Park as well as in a few well-treed neighborhoods. They are common along roadsides, sitting on power poles. Besides reddish undersides, their black and white barred wings and banded tail make them easy to recognize. They are also quite vocal, especially during courtship. With a screaming call variously described as a repeated *kee-yah* or *kee-ya*, they cannot be mistaken. Like most large hawks, they soar the skies, searching for a meal. Most of their prey consists of small mammals, but snakes are often eaten and occasionally insects or crayfish.

Soaring hawks are often called "buzzards" in other parts of the world while in the U.S. we use that name, incorrectly, for vultures.

As with most hawks, the female is larger than the male. In a nest 20 to 50 feet above ground both male and female guard the nest and incubate the eggs. After hatching, the female does most of the brooding of the young while the male does most of the hunting for the offspring. The eggs hatch asynchronously, so the oldest and biggest young get the first chance at the delivered food; in lean years the youngest hawks may starve. Being very neat, the young hawks at about five days of age lift their rear ends and eject feces out of the nest, minimizing infestations of parasites and bacteria.

Loss of riparian woodlands is a major cause of decline of this bird species. Red-shouldered Hawks prefer more wooded areas, especially around water, while the Red-tailed Hawks favor drier and more open locales.

Red-tailed Hawk
UPPER & LOWER PARK

From Canada to Panama and Atlantic to the Pacific, the Red-tailed Hawk is the most common and widespread of all North American raptors. The adult Red-tailed Hawk is easily identified as it leaves its perch with regular wing beats. Soaring in the sky, the broad, rounded tail shows a rusty red color, which gives the bird its name, but until they are about four years old, the tail is a banded brown.

Different Red-tailed Hawks vary from light to dark in coloration, but both adults and immature are identified by a dark belly band darker than the chest. About 19 inches in length and with a four foot wingspan, the female is about a third larger than the male, as is the case with most hawks.

A male and female, sometimes several, participate in elaborate courtship displays, soaring and calling, grasping each other's talons, and participating in other aerial maneuvers. Nesting in tall trees with nearby open areas for feeding, they lay three eggs which hatch asynchronously, resulting in three chicks of different ages and sizes. If food is abundant that breeding season, all chicks will fledge from the nest; if food is scarce only the one or two chicks will survive. They feed mainly on small mammals such as voles or field mice which they can spot with their excellent eyesight from over 100 feet away. Soaring hawks have an "eyeshade" formed by a piece of cartilage over their eyes, facilitating their vision but also giving them a bit of an ominous appearance. They will swallow small prey whole but dismember larger prey; they then regurgitate pellets containing indigestible parts such as teeth, bones, and hair.

The Red-tailed Hawk is a significant symbol in Native American culture and its feathers are used in religious ceremonies.

Once called the "chicken hawk" it was shot by farmers and ranchers in great numbers, even though it rarely preyed on chickens.

The Birds of Bidwell Park

American Kestrel
UPPER & LOWER PARK

The American Kestrel is one of the most common raptors from northern North America to southern South America. Found throughout the U.S. all year, it inhabits open areas such as grasslands, farm fields, deserts, meadows, and suburbia, where it is seen on power lines, fence posts, trees along the sides of roads and on highway meridians. About 8.5 inches long with a wingspan of 21 inches, this small, long-tailed hawk, actually a falcon, has a short, dark, hooked beak, long, narrow pointed wings, a gray crown with black spots at the side rear, white cheeks, and black mustache marks. Unlike most raptors, the sexes of the Kestrel can be distinguished in the field: the male has blue-tinged wing feathers and a rusty tail with a wide black band followed by a narrow white terminal band; the female lacks the bluish tinge and her rust-brown tail has numerous dark bars of even width and a narrow band at the end. It is certainly one of the most colorful raptors in the world. Its voice is a high-pitched *klee, klee, klee*.

"Kestrel" comes from a 15th-century French word meaning "crackle" or "rattle", referring to the sound the bird makes.

Kestrels typically hunt from a perch or by hovering over open areas, feeding mainly on small mammals and insects but they also eat small birds, especially slow moving House Sparrows. This gave them their original common name "Sparrow Hawk." The American Kestrel nests in tree cavities, old woodpecker holes, on buildings, nest boxes or old nests of other birds. Females lay three to seven eggs with incubation taking 29-30 days. The young kestrels fly about 30 days after hatching. American Kestrels are found all through Bidwell Park, especially in open areas. In addition to requiring open space for hunting, American Kestrels need perches for hunting and cavities for nesting.

The American Kestrel is the only North American falcon to hover with rapid wing beats and a motionless head while scanning the ground for prey, gliding with flat wings and its wingtips curved upward. It occasionally soars in circles with its tail spread and its wings flattened.

California Quail
UPPER & LOWER PARK

The California Quail, the official state bird, was for a time rather rare in Bidwell Park, primarily due to a large population of feral cats. After the removal of nearly 1,000 cats by the Chico Cat Coalition, the birds are once again common throughout the park in open forest, forest edges, and grassland. The California Quail is a short, rounded bird with a short black beak standing about nine inches tall; the male has a black throat, gray chest, and a topknot drooping forward. The female is much lighter in color, lacks the black throat and has a smaller topknot. You will frequently see them running across the road, rarely flying and then only for short distances.

Occasionally called the valley quail, the California Quail lives in a variety of habitats – grasslands, savannahs, woodlands, and the edge of deserts, wherever there is sufficient cover for them. These birds are gregarious and may live in coveys of ten to one hundred birds outside of the breeding season. These coveys often participate in communal dustbaths, using their undersides to loosen soil down an inch or two. They then wiggle and flap their wings to cover themselves with dust. The dust, like talcum powder, serves to dry the skin and feathers, preventing parasites from thriving, soothing skin irritations, and aligning feather barbs.

The distinctive topknot of the quail is actually composed of five or six individual feathers.

California Quail feed on the ground on seeds, leaves, flowers, and insects. Their intestines contain protozoan microorganisms that help digest the tough cellulose in these foods; the young quail obtain these protozoans by eating the droppings of the adults. Although quail typically walk or run, they will fly short distances and fly up into trees to roost. Like many birds that nest on the ground, the nest site is well hidden in the foliage and the dull-colored female tends to it.

Their distinctive call sounds to some like *Chi-ca-go*, *Chi-ca-go*, and the male and female often alternate singing, one following the other, a phrase at a time.

Wild Turkey
UPPER PARK

Wild Turkeys are thinner than domestic turkeys, with tails tipped with brown, not white. When Europeans colonized America they brought with them a domesticated stock of turkeys that they had bred from the Wild Turkey of North America. It is the only wild bird in North American that has been domesticated. Wild Turkeys were introduced into upper Bidwell Park in the 1970s and are doing well.

Wild Turkeys live in open woodlands and forests with clearings and meadows, traveling in flocks during the day looking for food such as insects, snails, salamanders, small lizards, frogs, millipedes, small snakes, worms, flowers, acorns, buds, and fruits, often by scratching the ground or climbing shrubs and small trees to feed. They often feed in cow pastures and even around backyard bird feeders. For most of the year, flocks of 20-30 are predominantly one sex, females with females, males with males but young turkeys of both sexes follow their mothers. The male has a spectacular display to attract females. He struts and gobbles, holding his tail vertically fanned out and wings spread and lowered. He produces low thumping sounds while he vibrates his tail. Males are polygamous, so they form territories that may have as many as five hens within them. Male Wild Turkeys display for females by puffing out their feathers, spreading out their tails and dragging their wings. This behavior is most commonly referred to as strutting.

Male turkey's heads and necks are colored brilliantly with red, blue and white. The color can change with the turkey's mood, with a solid white head and neck indicating a high level of excitement.

Male turkeys can grow to four feet in length; they sport black-tipped breast feathers while the females' are brown. Males also have a "beard" made of modified feathers that hang over the breast. Beards may be nine inches or more and a few females have a beard, usually shorter and thinner than that of the male. The adult male weighs 10-24 pounds and the female about half that.

Gulls
UPPER & LOWER PARK

Gulls are often referred to as "seagulls" but this name is not appropriate as all their common names use "gull" only and many are inland birds. Gulls are able to inhabit salt water as they have a pair of glands above their eyes specifically designed to flush the salt from their systems through openings in the bill. Sneezing is their way of eliminating salt from their system.

All gulls are opportunistic feeders and will eat most anything they can handle, but prefer to feed around water – ponds, lakes, marshes, and rivers where they find insects, fish, frogs, eggs of other birds, and will feed at garbage dumps. In fact, over half of their diet derives from scavenging. Gulls will steal food from each other, a trait called kleptoparasitsm.

Gulls are very intelligent and adaptable and have taken advantage of many human-created or influenced environments such as airports and garbage dumps. In the park, they are found around Horseshoe Lake, the golf course, lawns, ball fields, and other open areas. They are very social but keep their personal distance from each other.

These gulls winter on the Pacific Coast. The California Gull passes through Chico in the spring on its way to breeding grounds in the north, often in large flocks. The Herring and Ring-billed may be seen in the winter in the park. To tell them apart, look for a red and black spot on the lower bill, yellow legs, and dark eyes on the medium-sized California Gull. The larger Herring Gull has only a red spot on the bill, yellow eye, and pink legs, and the smaller Ring-billed Gull has a black ring around the bill, a light-colored eye, and yellow legs. Immature gulls have brownish or grayish plumage and are very difficult to distinguish.

In early June of 1848, thousands of California gulls arrived in Utah to eat hordes of "Mormon Crickets", which were destroying the settler's crops. A "Seagull Monument" was erected in Salt Lake to commemorate this event.

The Birds of Bidwell Park

American Coot
UPPER PARK

The American Coot is one of those birds that you will see anywhere that you might see waterfowl. It is not a duck but is actually related to rails and cranes. Its blackish body, shaped more like a chicken's than a duck's, yellow legs, and white bill, tell it from anything else except maybe the related but less abundant Common Moorhen, which has a red bill and brownish wings. Both birds are at home in the water but have lobed toes instead of webbed feet. Their feet are not particularly efficient and require a long takeoff from the water to acquire flight; often their taxi run is so long that they just settle down in the water again, going as far as they needed to.

Coots, sometimes called "mud hens" will eat vegetation, snails, and other invertebrates and are not above stealing from other coots. Unlike most other members of their family, they are not at all secretive and are easy to spot swimming or walking on vegetation in the water or on land. In the winter they are often seen in large flocks. Their somewhat mechanical and nasal *kuk-kuk-kuk-kuk* call is heard frequently as these birds are rather aggressive and territorial in the breeding season. They build a floating nest of reeds, cattails, and other vegetation, perhaps interspersed with floating plastic and cardboard, although the nests are often destroyed by muskrats. The red-billed young coots are able to swim shortly after hatching and can dive a month later. In the winter, coots are prey for a variety of hawks and carnivorous mammals. By some estimates, coots can be a major part of Bald Eagles' diets – up to 80%!

In Bidwell Park, Horseshoe Lake is about the only place you are likely to see American Coots, along with Canada Geese and a number of domestic duck and geese hybrids.

Hunters disdain this awkward, hesitant-to-fly-bird, perhaps leading to the term "old coot" for an eccentric, lazy elderly person.

Killdeer
UPPER PARK

The most commonly seen shorebird all year around, the ten-inch Killdeer gets its name from the screeching call it makes when disturbed. Strikingly brown and white with two black breast bands and a red ring around the eye, it is inconspicuous because those breast bands break up the silhouette of the bird. In flight, rusty coloration can be seen in the tail. Although it is a shorebird, Killdeer are often found away from open water such as grassy and agricultural areas, golf courses and airfields.

The male Killdeer chooses a spot for a nest and calls continually until a female shows interest and mating takes place. They share in making a minimal nest, usually a simple depression in sand or gravel, even on flat rooftops and gravel roads and always lay four eggs. The eggs are placed pointed-side inward so they don't roll and if an egg is destroyed, the adults will often put a rock in its place. Both male and female take turns incubating. Killdeer are well known for their habit of distracting a predator approaching its nest by feigning a broken wing and running away from the nest, sometimes also limping on a "broken" leg. The predator, seeing an easy meal, follows the adult and is rudely surprised when the broken wing act ends and the adult flies off. A close relative in Europe, the Lapwing, gets its name from that same behavior. The precocious Killdeer young are small balls of fluff, unable to fly, but able to feed themselves shortly after hatching, although their parents watch over them for a month until they become independent. Their food consists mainly of insects but they will also take small crustaceans and occasionally berries.

Baby killdeer hatch with their eyes open, and as soon as their downy feathers dry, they start to search the ground for their first meal.

Found mostly in the upper park in grassy areas, roadsides, Horseshoe Lake edges, and the golf course, often in small groups in the winter.

The Birds of Bidwell Park

Rock Pigeon
UPPER & LOWER PARK

The Rock Pigeon, formerly Rock Dove, is variously called "city pigeon", "feral pigeon", "homing pigeon", "carrier pigeon", or just plain pigeon. A European native, it has been introduced elsewhere and is found in cities all over the world. Preferring open habitats and rock ledges, it often roosts and nests on brick buildings, regularly making a pest of itself, sometimes earning the title of "winged rat". Rock Pigeons in the wild are pale gray and have two black wing bars but domestic and feral pigeons come in a variety of colors and patterns.

The Rock Pigeon has associated with humans for over 5000 years and has been bred for various reasons – show pigeons, carrier pigeons, racing pigeons – into over 200 varieties. In medieval Europe and the middle east, people built dovecotes to house and breed Rock Pigeons for their eggs and flesh and their feces for fertilizer. Pigeons are intelligent and have been used to discover clues to birds' navigational abilities and their ability to discern color.

Rock Pigeons are most common in areas such as ball fields, and parking lots, and adjacent buildings. They eat seeds, grain, invertebrates, and a variety of human leftovers such as bread, popcorn, and ice cream cones. Watch a pigeon drink: members of the pigeon family are the only birds that are able to suck up water from a source; all other birds have to fill their beaks and tip their heads up to swallow.

Other pigeon-like birds you might see are the similar Band-tailed Pigeon which is consistent in color across the birds in a group, has a banded tail and a white crescent on the nape, and the Mourning Dove, which is much smaller, with a pointed tail.

There is no biological difference between doves and pigeons, although those named pigeons tend to be larger. "Dove" comes from Anglo-Saxon and "pigeon" from French. The extinct Passenger Pigeon was so named after French explorers dubbed it "pigeon de passage" because of the huge size of migratory flocks that passed overhead.

Band-tailed Pigeon
UPPER PARK

Resembling the common non-native Rock Pigeon of cities, the Band-tailed Pigeon is a larger native bird with an iridescent nape, a white crescent on the back of its neck, and a wide light gray band on the end of its tail. The Rock Pigeon has a shorter tail and usually displays a white rump patch. The Band-tailed Pigeon is relatively quiet for a pigeon, with a low-pitched and owl-like call.

Preferring higher elevations in mixed and coniferous forests, the Band-tailed Pigeon is usually seen only in the Upper Park. It feeds on seeds, berries, and especially acorns. It is very social and feeds and moves in small flocks, usually from tree to tree but occasionally on the ground. It is a permanent resident in Chico, close to the north end of its winter range. Birds breeding farther north may migrate south to the park for the winter.

Loose colonies often form with several pairs nesting together. Nests are usually located in trees, in a fork on a horizontal branch, or at the base of a branch against the trunk. Males collect the nesting material of twigs; females build the nest and then lay two eggs. After hatching, parents feed the young "pigeon milk", a protein and fat-rich liquid produced by sloughing off the lining of their crops. Band-tailed Pigeons may raise two to three broods per year. In the winter large flocks of pigeons may form as they follow the acorn crop.

Early in the last century large numbers of these birds were killed because they were thought to be crop pests. They are legally hunted today in California but the effect on their populations is unknown. In Mexico large numbers are also shot in while the migrating birds are on their wintering grounds.

> *A parasitic louse believed to have become extinct with the extinction of the Passenger Pigeon was recently discovered living on the Band-tailed Pigeon.*

Mourning Dove
UPPER & LOWER PARK

The Mourning Dove is named so because of its plaintive *woo-oo-oo* call, which is often mistaken for that of an owl. It is so distinctive that wildlife biologists actually census the birds' populations by listening for their call. It is occasionally called the Western Turtle Dove or Rain Dove and is one of the most abundant birds of North America, like its extinct cousin, the Passenger Pigeon, once was. Breeding up to six times a year, its populations withstand the take of 70 million birds annually by hunters. With a body size smaller than the Rock and Band-tailed Pigeons, the Mourning Dove has a longer and pointed tail and is a very fast flier.

Mourning Doves, like all pigeons and doves, always lay two eggs, never an exception. This is called "determinate laying". If an egg is destroyed or lost, no replacement egg will be laid.

The Mourning Dove inhabits a variety of open environments such as grasslands, farms, and sparsely wooded forests, foraging for seeds which it eats almost exclusively. After a courtship display by the male during which he flies in large circles, he then approaches the female, puffs out his breast feathers, struts, and coos. If the female accepts his advances, the pair will preen each other's feathers. Both the male and female participate in building a very simple nest of twigs and grass in a tree, always laying two eggs. The nest is so hastily built that the eggs can often be seen through the nesting material. Often, they will simply use the old nest of other birds such as robins. When the young hatch about two weeks later, they are fed on "pigeon milk", which is actually the sloughed-off lining of the crop and is high in protein and fat for quick growth. After three or four days, this milk is supplemented by seeds. After two more weeks, the young leave the nest.

Barn Owl
UPPER & LOWER PARK

The Barn Owl is the most abundant and widespread of all owls, found nearly throughout the world. These birds are closely associated with humans through their traditional use of barn lofts and church steeples as nesting sites. Other names are the Ghost Owl, Church Owl, Death Owl, Hissing Owl, Hobgoblin or Hobby Owl, White Owl, Night Owl, Rat Owl, Straw Owl, Barnyard Owl and Delicate Owl. The upperparts are light gray with numerous fine dark lines and scattered pale spots. The chest and belly are white with a few black spots; females have more spots than males and the more spots the females have, the more attractive they are to males, because, for some reason, highly spotted females have fewer parasites. This whitish-tan owl has a heart-shaped white facial disc with a brownish edge.

Generally nocturnal, its flight is noiseless due to the frayed wingtips of its flight feathers. The Barn Owl calls infrequently, the usual call being a rasping screech or scream which you might hear in the park after dark. When approached in its roosting hollow or nest, it makes hissing and rasping noises made by clicking the tongue. Barn Owls prefer to hunt small ground mammals. Voles are an important food item, as well are pocket gophers, shrews, mice, rats, bats, frogs, lizards, birds and insects. Prey are usually located by the owl's sensitive sense of hearing, partly due to its large, but hidden, external ears.

Barn Owls will nest any time during the year, depending on food supply. The majority of Barn Owls nest in tree hollows, old buildings, caves and well shafts. Three to six eggs are incubated for about a month. Barn Owls are short-lived birds with most dying in their first year of life, the average life expectancy being one or two years in the wild. The Barn Owl is found in virtually all habitats but much more frequently in open woodland, shrubland and chaparral than forested country.

Barn Owls were once considered symbols, omens, and parts of myths and superstitions. Nailing a Barn Owl to a door was supposed to ward off bad luck.

Great Horned Owl
UPPER & LOWER PARK

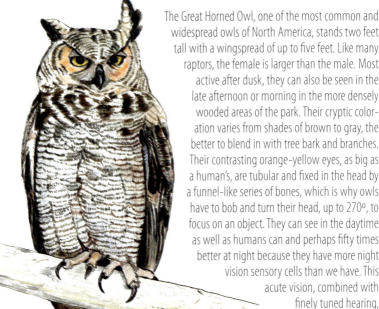

The Great Horned Owl, one of the most common and widespread owls of North America, stands two feet tall with a wingspread of up to five feet. Like many raptors, the female is larger than the male. Most active after dusk, they can also be seen in the late afternoon or morning in the more densely wooded areas of the park. Their cryptic coloration varies from shades of brown to gray, the better to blend in with tree bark and branches. Their contrasting orange-yellow eyes, as big as a human's, are tubular and fixed in the head by a funnel-like series of bones, which is why owls have to bob and turn their head, up to 270º, to focus on an object. They can see in the daytime as well as humans can and perhaps fifty times better at night because they have more night vision sensory cells than we have. This acute vision, combined with finely tuned hearing, made possible by ears of slightly different shape and locations on the head, allows them to locate sounds with amazing precision.

The "horns" are actually feather tufts; they help to camouflage the bird and their position indicates the mood of the owl.

Great Horned Owls hunt their small vertebrate prey by diving from their perch with wings folded, silently soaring over the ground, or even walking on the ground, to capture and devour small mammals, birds, reptiles, and even fish from shallow water. They grasp the prey with their talons and impale and crush them, with almost ten times the force of a human hand. Like all birds, they cannot chew their food and simply swallow large pieces, and like most owls, they regurgitate oblong balls of undigested feathers, fur, and bones, allowing anyone to collect these "owl pellets" from under the owl's roost and tease the pellets apart to determine the diet of a particular owl. The many species of owls vary in their calls but the *whoo-hoo-hoo* of the Great Horned Owl is the classic call we all know.

Western Screech Owl
UPPER & LOWER PARK

The Western Screech Owl was once part of a larger species, the Screech Owl, with a western and eastern population. It is one of the west's more common Owls at lower elevations. They are small (about nine inches), squat-looking owls that sit erect with fluffed out plumage, and their ear tufts raised. The iris and toes are yellow, contrasting with their mainly grayish or reddish-brown plumage which resembles tree bark, helping to camouflage them.

The call of the male is a constant *hoo-hoo-hoo* that speeds up in frequency, like a bouncing ball slowing down. During courtship males and females call in a duet as they get closer and when they meet they preen each other's head feathers. Western Screech Owls nest almost exclusively in tree cavities. They prefer natural cavities but will nest in the old holes created by Pileated Woodpeckers or Northern Flickers. They will also nest in nest boxes of appropriate sizes.

Western Screech Owls feed on a variety of prey. They favor voles, deer mice, larger insects, or small birds depending on abundance. Prey species also include shrews, moles, insects (including grasshoppers, beetles, larval moths & butterflies), birds, gophers, salamanders, bats, frogs, crayfish, worms, snails, and fish. Small prey is usually swallowed whole, later producing pellets, while large prey is shredded and swallowed on the spot.

Screech owls live and breed in a variety of habitats, and especially like lowland riparian sites and deciduous woodlands. They are non-migratory and can be seen in Bidwell Park, and the city, the year round. If you want to see them, your best chance is to walk along Big Chico Creek in the early evening at dusk or even later.

When threatened, the bird stretches out and flattens its feathers to look like a tree branch, but will fly off when a predator approaches too closely.

Common Nighthawk
UPPER PARK

The robin-sized Common Nighthawk is rare in Bidwell Park and most of the valley of California. But it is a fascinating bird you may see in the summer in the upper part of the park as one approaches the foothills. The nighthawk is not a hawk and it does not come out at night — it is crepuscular — it is most active at dusk and dawn; its large eyes allow good vision in poor light. It belongs to a very interesting group of birds which includes such species as oilbirds, potoos, nightjars and the whip-poor-will. The nighthawk belongs to a family called "goatsuckers" because its members were once thought to suck on goats' teats. The Common Nighthawk is a cryptic bird most often seen in flight, easily identified by the white bar across each long, pointed wing. Mottled gray and black, the bird has a tiny beak with a large gape which it uses to scoop up insects into its large sticky mouth. After enough insects get entrapped in the fly-paper like mouth, the bird swallows them.

The nighthawk's feet are so small and weak that the birds perch along a branch rather than across it as most birds do.

During the breeding season, males perform spectacular display flights, flying high up in the air with their seemingly erratic wing beats and then diving, ending with a booming noise as they open their wings and pull out of a fast dive. Because of this low-pitched call, they have been called "bullbats." Vocalizations also include a loud, distinctive call, given in flight as a short *peet* usually heard overhead. Originally nesting on open ground along rivers or other stretches of gravel, the Common Nighthawk sometimes nests on gravel rooftops in urban environments. The two eggs are laid directly on sand or gravel and no nest is built. It winters in South America.

Vaux's Swift
UPPER & LOWER PARK

Although the Vaux's Swift is not common in Bidwell Park, it is an interesting bird so it is included here. Swifts are very aerial birds, similar to swallows in appearance but are only distantly related. Swifts are actually more closely related to hummingbirds. But both swifts and swallows make a living by catching insects in flight.

The family name, Apodidae, means "without feet". Swifts do have feet but almost never alight on the ground, preferring to perch on vertical surfaces such as cave walls, cliffs, and chimneys instead. Chinese birds-nest soup is derived from the nests of Cave Swifts in Asia which use saliva to construct their nests.

The Vaux's Swift is usually seen only in flight and is distinguished by a very short tail, the ends of the feather shafts sticking out like bristles. This five inch bird is often described as a brownish-gray cigar with long, narrow, crescent-shaped wings and a rapid flight. In flight the swift's wings appear to flap in a stiff and alternate fashion, which distinguishes swifts from swallows that have a more coordinated wing beat.

Townsend, a zoologist who discovered many new species of animals, named this bird after William Vaux, a 19th century mineralogist. Townsend himself has a warbler and solitaire named after him.

Butte County is at the southernmost limit of their breeding range and the northernmost limit of their winter range, but they are most often seen in the spring over open areas such as the golf course and Horseshoe Lake, catching insects in the early morning or late evening.

Swifts naturally roost in caves or natural crevices, but in recent times have taken up the habit of using chimneys for their evening retreats. They have short legs and weak feet, but all four toes face forward to help them hold onto the vertical surface of the chimney.

Anna's Hummingbird
UPPER & LOWER PARK

The Anna's Hummingbird is the only North American hummingbird with a totally red head. The feathers of the male's head are iridescent, a result of feather structure, but can appear black or green in different light conditions. The rest of the body is grayish green with a white-tipped tail. Females and immature birds are difficult to distinguish from other species but the Anna's is by far the most common hummingbird in Bidwell Park all year around. Their rapid flight, vibrating wings, hovering, and feeding on flowers make these four-inch birds easy to spot.

Named after a French Duchess, the Anna's has expanded its California range northward with the development of suburban homes and gardens. They feed on nectar much of the year, dipping their brush-like tongue into the neck of a flower, sopping it up and pulling the tongue into the beak to squeeze out the concentrated sugar water. They are very territorial both summer and winter, defending their food supply vigorously. Field observations have shown that territories around nectar producing flowers are established very quickly and the boundaries are changed as the nectar supply changes. Look for them on Manzanita shrubs when they flower. A hummingbird feeder, with a constant food supply, may attract many individuals, all of whom try to defend it against intruders, usually not very successfully as a sugar feeder is very attractive to hummingbirds.

Although hummingbirds are known for drinking nectar, they are voracious insect eaters during the breeding season as young birds need protein which insects have and nectar does not.

The male has a thin and buzz-like courtship song. While courting, the male performs a display dive at up to 50 mph. When he pulls out of the dive he spreads his wings and tail, resulting in a loud kind of squeak and boom. The female raises the young alone in a nest she builds of fine materials such as moss and lichen held together by spider silk.

Belted Kingfisher
UPPER & LOWER PARK

The Belted Kingfisher is most often seen flying along or above Big Chico Creek as it makes its distinctive, raucous, chattering call, but it can also be spotted above any body of water as it searches for likely prey. It plunges into the water headfirst to capture fish, its preferred food, but it will also take frogs, crustaceans, small mammals, and large insects. Kingfishers typically hover before diving vertically into the water although they rarely go under. If successful, they will return to their perch and beat the fish or other prey against a branch to soften it. Sometimes they will throw the prey into the air to reorient it for easier swallowing. Like owls and hawks, kingfishers regurgitate pellets of indigestible material. Kingfishers require fairly clear water in order to see their prey so they are more common along Big Chico Creek than around the usually turbid Horseshoe Lake.

A medium-sized bird, its shaggy crest and large head make it nearly impossible to confuse with any other bird in park. Both male and female have a crest, are grayish blue on the back, and the wings and head and have a band of gray across their white underparts. Belted Kingfishers show reverse sexual dimorphism, meaning that the female is more brightly colored than the male as she has a rusty colored band, or "belt," across her lower belly.

The two outer toes of the kingfisher are fused together; this arrangement allows them to be more efficient at tunnel digging.

Belted Kingfishers are usually seen by themselves except during breeding season. After pairing up, the male and female spend nearly a week excavating a tunnel, up to eight feet long, in the sandy or clay bank of a river or stream at the end of which five to eight eggs are laid. The parents feed the young regurgitated food for about a month after hatching and then lead the young out of the burrow. But it is another three weeks before they can feed on their own. The tunnel is mostly horizontal but slopes upward to minimize the possibility of flooding.

Acorn Woodpecker
UPPER & LOWER PARK

Signs of the Acorn Woodpecker are all over the park. Just look for trees that have numerous thumb-size holes in them. These are called "granary trees," and the holes were made by Acorn Woodpeckers in order to store acorns. The birds hammer the acorns into the holes and when they want to eat the nut, they come back and peck the shell open. Wedging acorns into these holes deters crows, jays, squirrels and others from burglarizing the acorn cache. Fresh acorns dry out and shrink, so the birds have to maintain the granary by moving the acorns to smaller holes later. The birds will also eat tree sap and the insects attracted to it; they also sally out from a perch to catch flying insects in mid-air and forage for berries and seeds.

Native Americans of California used the Acorn Woodpeckers and their acorns for food and for feathers to decorate vests and headdresses.

Acorn Woodpeckers live in small groups as an extended family with six to a dozen or more members. The birds excavate a cavity in a dead tree or tree branch and build a simple nest within. There may only be one pair in a group of birds or several males and females that mate indiscriminately with each other. It is not unusual to find a nest with eggs that have different sets of parents. When the young hatch, the parents may be assisted in their feeding by all the members of the group.

A medium-sized woodpecker, the adult is black on the back and wings and throat with a white forehead, underside and upper base of the tail. The adult male has a red cap with a creamy white forehead and throat. The female has a smaller red cap with a black forehead and white below.

Found all year anywhere there are an abundance of oak trees, you will often see these woodpeckers displaying with their outstretched wings and calling with a distinctive *nyaah, nyaah, nyaah* call.

Nuttall's Woodpecker
UPPER & LOWER PARK

The Nuttall's Woodpecker is a small woodpecker, a little more than seven inches long. Like most woodpeckers, it is mostly black and white; it has a series of bars across its back and wings, and a black tail. The male has a red patch on his head. The nine-inch Acorn Woodpecker is larger with a black back, the six and a half inch Downy Woodpecker has a white stripe on its back and the eight and a half-inch Red-breasted Sapsucker has a white stripe on the wing.

The Nuttall's Woodpecker is restricted to California and northern Mexico west of the Sierra Nevada and Cascade ranges. They can be found throughout the park wherever oak trees are found. Although Nuttall's Woodpeckers prefer to forage in oak trees, they do not eat acorns, but prefer fruits, berries, and insects, especially adult and larval beetles. They work their way carefully across trunks and branches searching crevices and under the bark, often hanging upside down as they forage, flaking and probing the bark rather than drilling.

All woodpeckers "drill" or peck at the bark of trees for three reasons: to make noise, called "drumming", in order to declare their territory; to drill a hole for a nest; or to look for insects or sap to eat. They have a special mechanism in their jaws to prevent jarring their brains. They are able to hold onto the tree firmly while pecking because they have two toes forward and two toes back (most birds have three forward and one back), and their tail feathers are stiffened with a heavy quill. Woodpeckers also have bristle-like feathers covering their nostrils so that they do not breathe in wood chips while pecking.

Thomas Nuttall was an English naturalist who spent many years in the U.S. collecting specimens; this woodpecker was named after him by William Gambel (after whom a quail is named).

Northern Flicker
UPPER & LOWER PARK

The Northern Flicker is a woodpecker, but an unusual one. It is larger than average at over 12 inches, is brown, gray and spotted rather than black and white, and is the only woodpecker that commonly feeds on the ground. The underside of the wings and tail vary from yellow to red and every color in between, with most yellow birds being eastern and red ones being found in the western U.S., leading ornithologists for years to think they were different species. They are now all called Northern Flickers. Their shape, size, and behavior are distinctive as is their call, *ki-ki-ki-ki*, sort of a Woody Woodpecker kind of laugh. It is easy to tell the sexes of the Northern Flicker apart — the male has the red mustache. They are year-round residents and will peck rapidly on hollow trees to make a reverberating sound to declare their nesting or feeding territories. They will even peck on metal power or light posts if they can create an even louder sound.

Flickers are "indeterminate layers" — they will replace any eggs in their nest if one is destroyed or eaten by a predator so that they have a clutch size of five to eight eggs.

Like all woodpeckers, they will peck on trees in search of insects and their larvae, and will make holes in hollow structures for a nest entrance. Flickers are often the bane of owners of wood or wood-shingled homes as they will make holes in those as well. They have even been known to peck through metal patches over holes in the wooden house!

They feed on the ground in open areas, eating almost any food material, but they often prefer ants. They not only eat ants, but crush them and rub them through their feathers as the ants' formic acid protects the skin and feathers from parasites; this behavior is called "anting" and is common among a number of birds.

Red-breasted Sapsucker
UPPER & LOWER PARK

The Red-breasted Sapsucker is a special kind of woodpecker. Usually seen only in the winter in Bidwell Park as it nests at higher elevations, it occasionally nests in streamside habitats. It is identified by its red head and breast, black back barred with white and a large white stripe on the wing. Most woodpeckers peck on dead or dying trees to extract the insects and their larvae in the tree. The sapsucker, however, prefers live trees in which it drills a series of small holes in a semi-organized pattern of parallel holes, giving the tree the appearance of being machine-gunned by a very small gangster. The bird leaves while the tree oozes sap. When the sapsucker returns, it feeds on both the sap and the insects that are attracted to it.

All woodpeckers have a specialized tongue supported by a series of bones that wrap around the jaw and over the top of the head. This allows the birds to extend their tongue far out of their bill to reach food in crevices or holes. The sapsucker's tongue is also fringed along its front portion, the hairlike fringes acting like a mop to soak up the sap. Hummingbirds will make use of these sap wells and eat the sap and insects attracted to it as well. Appropriately, a group of sapsuckers is known as a "slurp". Red-breasted Sapsuckers will eat berries as well, including those of poison oak, elderberries, dogwood, and pepper tree. They will eat a variety of insects including flying ones and occasionally their diet will be dominated by ants and their larvae.

The Red-breasted Sapsuckers nest primarily in conifers or soft deciduous trees such as cottonwood or aspen. Four or five eggs are laid in a nest simply made of wood chips from the nest excavation.

Young sapsuckers spend several weeks with the parents learning how to drill sap wells.

Black Phoebe
UPPER & LOWER PARK

The Black Phoebe is very common all throughout Bidwell Park and any place in Chico where water is nearby. Although it is an insect eater that you would suspect would only be around during the summer, it is actually around all year, aggressively defending a territory. To supplement its insect diet, it can catch small fish. A distinctive bird about seven inches long with a black head, breast and back, contrasting with a white abdomen, wing linings and outer tail feathers, it exhibits a characteristic flipping and wagging tail motion.

Very easy to find and observe, you can frequently see Black Phoebes flying out from a low perch to capture a flying insect, only to return to that perch or a nearby one in a few seconds. Their quick-closing jaws are capable of capturing the fastest insects.

The phoebe's name comes from its sharp "fee-bee" call.

The female hovers over a preferred nest site, usually something on a wall, bridge or cliff, always near water, and the male responds by starting construction on a mud and grass or straw nest stuck to the side of some structure; the female then takes over and finishes the building. An old name for this bird was the "bridge pewee" because of its preference for over-water structures. The pair lays three to six eggs which hatch about two weeks after incubation begins; the young leave the nest in about two more weeks. The phoebe appears to benefit from human activities and structures by feeding along irrigation ditches, artificial ponds and nesting on buildings and bridges. Black Phoebes also seem to have a great tolerance for human activities and habitations. The drying up of natural water sources will likely lead to the increased usage of human habitats by Black Phoebes. This species has an estimated global population of 970,000 individuals, a healthy population, considering that many birds' populations are declining.

Ash-throated Flycatcher
UPPER & LOWER PARK

The Ash-throated Flycatcher is found in Bidwell Park during the summer breeding season, spending the colder months in Mexico or Central America. It arrives in Chico about the end of April and leaves in late summer. About eight inches long, it can be identified by its grayish chest and throat, yellow belly, brown back, and a rusty color in the wings and tail. Like all flycatchers, it can erect a short crest on its head when excited. The male and female are similar in their plumage.

Like all flycatchers, this species is primarily an insectivore but will eat berries in winter when insects are scarce. Most of the time Ash-throated Flycatchers sit nearly motionless. When foraging, they perch on a branch and fly out in short bursts to glean prey from low foliage, branches, and the ground. Unlike most flycatchers in their family, they move from perch to perch when feeding, rather than returning to the same perch. Their foraging flights seem effortless, like a solo avian ballet. If an insect is large or hard-bodied, the birds will beat the insect body on a branch with sideways swipes of their head until the insect is somewhat softened. Because their food items contain moisture, Ash-throated Flycatchers almost never drink.

Flycatchers in North America belong to the family Tyrannidae, *so called because of the birds' aggressive tendencies.*

This flycatcher prefers open woodland or shrub where the nest is built in a tree cavity or artificial cavity, and normally produces a clutch of three or four eggs. The male defends a territory around the nest and announces it with calls that can be described as *che-whit* or *brzz*. Both members of the pair help build the nest of twigs, rootlets, and weeds and line it with soft feathers, fine grasses and hair or fur. The female usually deposits four buff brown eggs with brown splotches. The eggs hatch after about two weeks of incubation and the young leave the nest in about another two weeks, a process called fledging. The young are not good fliers when they leave the nest so the parents care for them for about another two weeks.

Western Kingbird
UPPER & LOWER PARK

The Western Kingbird is often found perched on roadside fences as it searches for insects. Aggressive birds, they fiercely defend their nests and young, often driving away crows, ravens, and hawks. Western Kingbirds have adapted extremely well to the presence of humans, and sometimes are found nesting within urban areas. They winter in Mexico, Central America, and Florida, and arrive in Chico in early April. At eight to nine inches long, slightly larger than the Ash-throated Flycatcher, the head and back are colored pale gray, with a white neck and yellow underparts and white outer tail feathers which are usually only seen in flight.

Western Kingbirds inhabit semi-open terrain with scattered trees and are often seen on solitary trees, fence posts, or fence wires. The male, during courtship, twists and turns high in the air, then stalls, tumbles, flips, and twists as he descends to attract a female. Kingbirds will nest on artificial structures when trees are not available. They lay four eggs which they incubate for nearly three weeks. Fledging occurs in 16-17 days. The nest is made from sticks and lined with plant fiber and usually built in a tree or bush.

This kingbird's scientific name is Tyrannus verticalis, reflecting the ramrod straight posture they often assume.

Western Kingbirds prefer insects as their main diet but they will also take fruits and berries. They typically feed by scanning from a perch, and flying out to catch insects in mid-air, in typical flycatcher fashion called "hawking" or "sallying". They also are very capable of hovering, dropping down to catch prey when spotted. The Western Kingbird is one of the few birds that has benefited from the cutting of forests. Agricultural lands with hay and livestock pastures provide a plentiful diet of insects and a lot of barbed wire to perch on. Kingbirds reflect their name with their aggressiveness, even defending their territory against hawks.

Loggerhead Shrike
UPPER & LOWER PARK

Unless one is a birdwatcher, the Loggerhead Shrike is not a familiar bird and its name does not seem descriptive. "Loggerhead" refers to the bulbous head shape, which looks like the old tool used to melt metal or tar; "shrike" derives from the shrieking call the bird makes. The shrike resembles a mockingbird but is slightly smaller with a shorter tail, more compact head, hooked bill, and large black stripe through the eye. It is a year-round resident and is most often seen on barbed-wire fences and nearby perches such as fence posts or bare tree branches near grasslands or wetlands.

The Loggerhead Shrike is both a songbird and a true predator with a sharp hooked beak although it does not have the talons of a raptor. It catches relatively large prey such as grasshoppers and beetles, shrews, mice, lizards, frogs and even small birds. When hunting, shrikes usually swoop down from their perch, hover or flutter close to the ground looking for prey, and then land on another perch. Interestingly, it impales its captures on the thorns of thorny bushes, or, more often, on the barbs of barbed wire. It may eat its prey immediately after shredding it while it hangs on the barb or leave it hang for awhile, especially if it is poisonous prey such as caterpillars or butterflies. This is an evolutionary compensation for not having sharp talons to hold prey with. A male may have five or more items displayed on a fence in his territory in order to attract a female by demonstrating to her what an efficient hunter he is.

The shrike is often called the "butcher bird" and, rarely, the "French Mockingbird".

The Loggerhead Shrike is a threatened species in Canada and is declining in the U.S., apparently due to both habitat destruction and pesticide use. Its population has been reduced by 75% in the past 40 years. A related species, the Northern Shrike, is rarely seen in northern California.

Western Scrub Jay
UPPER & LOWER PARK

The Western Scrub Jay is a familiar bird of lowland forests, brushy areas, backyards, and bird feeders. The scrub jay, as its name implies, inhabits scrub and brushy areas but is common in parks, gardens, and backyards. These birds are common, especially in the lower park. Patterned in blue, gray, and white, these nearly foot-long birds are well known for their appearance, tameness, and raucous call. They feed on small animals such as insects, lizards, frogs, mammals and birds and in the winter, nuts, seeds and acorns. They will occasionally peck through the bottom of the nest of a nesting bird to eat the eggs or young birds. This behavior and their harsh call have given them a rather unsavory reputation.

Although the Scrub Jay is a blue jay, it is not the Blue Jay, a separate species, which lives east of the Rocky Mountains.

Like others of the jay and crow family, scrub jays are quite intelligent. They cache acorns in the soil, sometimes covering the burial site with a leaf, and remember where the caches are months later, enabled by one of the largest brain sizes in their family. They will also steal acorns from other jays' caches. If a jay notices another jay watching it bury its cache, the jay doing the burying will return later to move the cache in order not to be burglarized by the observing jay. Oak trees are dependent on birds and mammals for propagation as some acorns that are not retrieved germinate later.

Ranging throughout most of the non-desert lowlands of southwestern U.S., from Washington to Mexico and Colorado to coastal California islands, the species has several geographical subspecies with differences in coloration. A separate species, the Island Scrub Jay, evolved on Santa Cruz Island. Due to the increase in suburban homes with yards and gardens, the scrub jay is increasing in numbers and expanding its range. For unknown reasons, members of the jay and crow family are especially susceptible to the West Nile Virus.

Yellow-billed Magpie
UPPER & LOWER PARK

The almost crow-sized, strikingly patterned Yellow-billed Magpie is found only in the California Valley and southern California coastal regions. Like other members of the crow and jay family, magpies are omnivorous — they eat almost anything they find on the ground, although they prefer insects, especially grasshoppers, and will also eat fruit, nuts, acorns, and even roadkill or other carrion.

Yellow-billed Magpies prefer to nest in groves of tall trees along rivers and near open areas, but they will nest almost anywhere, building a large, dome-shaped nest nearly one yard across made of sticks and mud near the top of a tree. There may be many birds nesting in a colony. You will most often see them in the grasslands of upper Bidwell Park, but they are not unusual in the open areas of Lower Lark. They are found all year as they are non-migratory.

They are raucous, noisy, and gregarious birds, hopping around in a flock, seemingly having a good time. The name "magpie" comes from the English "Mag", short for Maggie or Margaret, referring to a woman who gossips. "Pie" comes from "piebald" or "pied" meaning patched, and referring to the patches of colors on the bird. The black, white, and iridescent blue of the bird sets off its bright yellow bill so it can't be mistaken for any other. They are close relatives of the Black-billed Magpie whose range covers much of the western U.S. outside of California.

Like other members of the crow and jay family, their numbers declined due to West Nile virus, but they are recovering. They are, however, suffering from a loss of habitat and exposure to chemicals such as herbicides and chemicals used to poison ground squirrels.

When a Yellow-billed Magpie dies, there may be a "funeral" of sorts, with other magpies gathering around the carcass, squawking and jumping around.

The Birds of Bidwell Park

Crow and Raven
UPPER & LOWER PARK

American Crow

Common Raven

The American Crow (left) is considered one of the most intelligent birds in the world because it is one of the few bird species in the world that uses tools to obtain food. It will drop acorns or other nuts on roadways and let cars crack the shells and use sticks to probe for food items in the soil. Numbering over 30 million in the U.S., it is considered a pest in some areas, especially when it eats crops, but atones for that behavior by eating large numbers of insect pests. Crows are totally black, 18 inches long, common in the open areas of Bidwell Park and can only be confused with the Common Raven (below), which is a heavier-bodied bird (about a third larger, nearly the size of a Red-tailed Hawk) and which is seen with increasing frequency in the park. Look for the crow's rounded tail and the raven's wedge-shaped one. Crows emit a variety of calls, but most of them sound like *caw*.

A group of American Crows is called a "murder" of crows from a 15th-century phrase, a "murther of crows" — simply a flock.

American Crows are omnivorous and will eat both plant and animal matter indiscriminately. In natural habitats they are found eating nuts, acorns, seeds, insects and worms; you may also see them at bird feeders, garbage dumps, and agricultural fields. Crows and other members of the crow and jay family store food in a "cache" for later use.

The West Nile virus is transmitted by mosquitoes and birds serve as a reservoir for the virus. Birds are variously susceptible to the virus but it appears that the crow, jay, and magpie family suffers from a 100 percent death rate. The populations of these species have dropped but apparently some virus-resistant individuals are surviving to build the populations back to their previous levels.

American Crows are monogamous but pairs may form large families of up to 15 individuals from several breeding seasons.

The Birds of Bidwell Park

Barn & Cliff Swallows
UPPER & LOWER PARK

The Barn Swallow (right) is the most widespread swallow in the world. It is about six inches long, blue above with a reddish belly, rusty throat and face, and most distinctively, a long, deeply forked tail and curved, pointed wings. There are several species of swallows in the Chico area, but the Barn Swallow is one of the most common and certainly the easiest to identify. The Barn Swallow inhabits open country and typically builds a cup-shaped nest on artificial structures and can nest anywhere there are open areas for foraging, a water source, and a sheltered ledge. They are found in open habitats of all types, including barns or other outbuildings and Horseshoe Lake is a good place to find them. They also build nests of mud and straw under bridges, the eaves of old houses, boat docks, caves and even on slow-moving trains. Barn Swallows form breeding pairs in the spring on their nesting grounds. The male courts the female by spreading his wings and singing. If the female finds the male attractive, they will mate in the air.

Barn Swallow

Aristotle created the myth — which persisted for 1,500 years — that swallows burrow in the mud of ponds and lakes for the winter and emerge from the water in the spring.

The similar Cliff Swallow (left) is distinguished from the Barn Swallow by its white forehead, pale collar and short tail. It makes mud nests under bridges, on eves of buildings, and other structures, scooping the mud up from shorelines of lakes or similar areas. Swallows are not very adept on land or perches but are excellent fliers and easily able to capture their insect food on the wing.

Cliff Swallow

Swallows leave the Chico area in the late summer or fall to winter in Central and South America, returning in mid-April. They migrate during the day, eating insects in mid-air en route, and may cover 600 miles on a favorable day. Because of their streamlined body and well-designed wings, swallows use 50-75% less energy flying than do most songbirds.

Tree & Violet-green Swallows
UPPER & LOWER PARK

Violet-green Swallow

Tree Swallow

Tree and Violet-green Swallows are similar in appearance, with greenish-tinged upper sides and are often found together. The Violet-green Swallow has a shiny deep green back while the Tree Swallows' upperparts are iridescent blue-green; both have white underneath and a slightly forked tail. They are most often seen flying so the easiest way to distinguish between them is to look for white extending above the eye and white sides above the rump in the Violet-green Swallow. Both species fly in flocks pursuing aerial insects. They will fly low over water and pick insects off the ground as well. Look for them mostly in open areas of upper park, especially Horseshoe Lake.

Swallows are seen occasionally fighting for feathers floating through the air. This could be competition for nesting material or just a form of play.

Both species nest in rock crevices, woodpecker holes in trees, old Cliff and Barn Swallow nests and readily use nest boxes. Tree and Violet-green Swallows will nest in colonies when possible but will nest as lone pairs as well. Disappearance of habitat, the felling of dead trees, and the replacement of wooden fences with fiberglass or plastic ones have made nesting holes scarce. In addition, woodpeckers are on the wane in some areas, so not as many natural tree holes are being made. European Starlings, wrens, bluebirds, nuthatches, and others compete for a declining number of nesting holes as well, making artificial next boxes very valuable.

Both Tree and Violet-green Swallows have been known to lay their eggs in the nest of a Bald Eagle pair. Since the swallows and eagle do not need the same resources, there is no competition, and the swallows benefit because they are protected from most kinds of predation as few predators will approach an eagle's nest.

Swallows leave the Chico area in the late summer or fall to winter in Central and South America, returning in mid-April.

Oak Titmouse
UPPER & LOWER PARK

The Oak Titmouse was once called the "Plain Titmouse" until it was discovered via DNA comparisons that it shared the name with a now different species, the "Juniper Titmouse". They appear identical and differ by their habitat and a slight variation in their calls, as well as DNA. The Oak Titmouse is the only titmouse in Bidwell Park, common anywhere there are oaks – mostly Lower Park and the forested area of Upper Park. Small, at nearly six inches, they are drab gray with a brownish tinge but easily distinguished by their profile which shows their topknot. You can also hear their loud and characteristic *peter, peter, peter* or *wheety, wheety, wheety* call which are most frequent during the breeding season in early spring. Trained observers can even tell individual birds apart by their calls.

The titmouse primarily nests in natural cavities in trees, often those made by woodpeckers, or it may nest in bluebird boxes. The female builds a nest in late February to April. Pairs stay together after the breeding season and some say titmice mate for life, but scant evidence exists to support that idea. Sudden Oak Death fungal disease has caused habitat loss for the Oak Titmouse though in the short term it could increase availability of nesting cavities because the disease produces more dead trees. However, efforts to prevent the spread of the oak pathogen often include removing all dead and infected trees.

Oak Titmice like to forage from a high branch and even if they fly down to the ground to pick up a meal, they will return to a high branch to eat it. Their food consists of berries, acorns, seeds, and a variety of insects and spiders, often taken in midair. Hard or large seeds or invertebrates are beaten on a branch until they are cracked open. The titmouse will visit bird feeders to feed on seeds, suet, and peanut butter.

Tittr was Old Icelandic for Titmouse; "tit" means "something small" in Old English and "mouse" is from "mose" which is from early German "maisa", meaning "little or tiny". So, a titmouse is a "tiny small."

Bushtit
UPPER & LOWER PARK

The Bushtit is one of the smallest songbirds in North America at four and one half inches long. It is gray-brown overall, with a large head, a short neck, a long tail, and a short stubby bill. The male has dark eyes and the female's are yellow. The Bushtit lacks major identifying markings, so it is often identified by its shape, calls, and behaviors. It is a permanent resident of Bidwell Park.

Very gregarious, Bushtits are active, foraging in mixed species flocks containing species such as chickadees and warblers with perhaps ten to forty individuals in a flock. Members of the group constantly contact each other with calls that can be described as a short *tsit*. In cold weather, the group may roost together to stay warm by sharing body heat. They glean insects, insect larvae, and insect eggs from leaves and twigs, often hanging upside down to get at the undersides of leaves. They will occasionally eat berries and seeds and sometimes visit suet feeders. In the spring, they pair off for breeding.

Bushtits were one of the first birds described as having "helpers at the nest," non-parents who help raise the young.

The nest is a woven, hanging basket with a hole on the high side of the nest leading to the nest chamber at the bottom. It may be a foot long, and is generally built of spider webs and other fine plant material. The nest may be lined with feathers, fur, and moss. Both parents incubate the four to ten eggs for 12-13 days, sometimes at the same time. Bushtit parents glue the eggs to the bottom of the nest with saliva so they are not damaged and the swinging of the nest in the wind substitutes for turning the eggs during incubation. Both brood the young and bring them food until shortly after they leave the nest at about 18 days. Sometimes there are helpers at the nest — birds other than the parents that help to feed the nestlings. They generally raise two broods a year.

White-breasted Nuthatch
UPPER & LOWER PARK

The White-breasted Nuthatch gets its name from its occasional try at opening a nut it has wedged into a tree crevice as if it were helping it to hatch. Most often you will see these little (five to six inches) birds heading down a tree, usually in a spiral pattern, as they probe the bark for insects and spiders and their eggs and larvae in the summer and search for seeds in the winter. With a gray back, white breast, black head and nape, and their vertically prone position, they are unmistakable. Like other nuthatches, their call is distinctive and loud for such a small bird. It is often described as a nasal *yank-yank-yank*.

The White-breasted Nuthatch is a permanent resident of Bidwell Park and usually nests in a natural hole in a tree, often one left by a woodpecker. The nest is typically 10-30 feet above the ground and lined with fur, fine grass, and shredded bark. Five to nine eggs are incubated by the female for two weeks and when the eggs hatch, both adults feed the chicks.

Being a small bird, the nuthatch has trouble keeping warm in the winter, so it often roosts in holes or under loose bark to preserve body heat, sometimes in groups of several birds. The nuthatch is unusual is that it cleans its roost by removing its feces each morning. The White-breasted Nuthatch may also congregate in small mixed flocks of nuthatches and titmice in the winter. Not only can these flocks roost together to share body heat, but their movement in flocks during the day helps them all to find food and detect predators.

Like most small birds, nuthatches only live about two to three years.

Nuthatches may smear beetles or ants around their nest entrance, the unpleasant smell from the crushed insects apparently deterring squirrels, a major nest site competitor.

Brown Creeper
UPPER & LOWER PARK

Brown Creeper sounds more like a comic book character than a bird, but this inconspicuous little bird belongs to an interesting guild of birds that make their living by pecking and probing in the crevices of tree bark for insects, their larvae and eggs, spiders, and other arthropods too small for most birds. Brown Creepers are uniquely adapted to this foraging style because of their long, thin, and curved bill for probing, long claws for adhering to the tree trunk, and stiffened tail feathers to support their bodies while climbing and probing. They typically fly to the bottom of a tree trunk and climb upwards in a spiral pattern. Although nuthatches creep like creepers, nuthatches have straight bills, short tails, and tend to start at the top of a tree and work their way down. The brown coloration with white streaking, white breast, and rufous tail are also distinctive Brown Creeper features and provide them some camouflage. They are small birds, about five inches long and weighing slightly over a quarter ounce, or about the weight of seven or eight paper clips.

Not only is the Brown Creeper inconspicuously colored, it will flatten itself against a tree trunk with wings spread to camouflage itself even further.

Brown Creepers are solitary birds outside of the breeding season, but in colder climes, a group of 20 or more birds, sometimes including nuthatches and chickadees as well, will form a communal roost in a tree cavity or crotch of a large branch and huddle closely together. Small birds lose body heat quite rapidly, so such roosting helps to prevent the excessive loss of body heat. They also need to eat continually during the daylight hours to store enough energy to make it through the night.

Resident in the winter and early spring in Bidwell Park, Brown Creepers move northwards or to higher elevations to breed. They make their nests behind coniferous tree bark which is hanging loose from tree trunks or branches, constructing them with twigs, bark, moss, and lichen and held together by spider webs.

Bewick's and House Wrens
UPPER & LOWER PARK

The Bewick's Wren (right) was once common throughout the East and Midwest a hundred years ago but is now restricted to the west and southwest. A little less than five inches long, Bewick's Wrens are slender with long tails, brown above and gray below. Their tails are barred with a bit of white at the outer tips. The most distinctive field mark of the Bewick's Wren is the bold white stripe over the eye. The House Wren (below) is plainer, with no eye stripe or spots on the tail, but with bolder wing barring.

Bewick's Wren

Both wrens inhabit the edges of forests throughout Bidwell Park and build nests of almost any material such as leaves, twigs, grass, moss, strips of bark and other such materials in natural cavities or in heavy brush. The males may build two or three trial nests from which the female chooses. They lay five to six speckled pinkish eggs which hatch about two weeks later. After two more weeks, the young fledge (leave the nest.) The Bewick's Wren feeds mainly on insects and spiders as well as other arthropods and forage by gleaning from the lower branches of trees or from shrubs; they occasionally eat the berries of elderberry and poison oak. The House Wren is more likely to nest near human habitation. The House and Bewick's Wren are in a bit of a competition for nest sites and food, but the decline of both species seems to have more to do with habitat destruction than competition.

House Wren

A wren pair may make up to 600 trips per day to feed their clutch of young birds.

The House Wren song is rich and melodious, increasing in pitch and volume and then trailing off. Bewick's Wrens songs are complex, consisting of trills and buzzes and not very melodic. Both birds' songs vary enormously. An individual male may sing 15 or more distinct songs which he learns from mature males in the area. A wren will repeat one song for almost two minutes, then switch to the next song.

American Dipper
UPPER PARK

This bird, once called a "water ouzel" but now named more descriptively as the American Dipper, has the habit of bobbing up and down by extending and straightening its knees. Although its body shape and size reminds one of a thrush with long legs and a short tail and certainly not a water bird, it is very aquatic and extremely agile in the rushing water of a stream. It actually flies underwater to depths of 20 feet and uses its strong legs to roll over rocks to capture the aquatic insect larvae hidden there, on which they feed almost exclusively. Less frequently, they will feed on small fish and fish eggs. Feeding as they do is like trying to eat in a washing machine! During times of peak insect emergence, dippers may be seen flying off on short round-trips after insects on the shore or skimming the newly emerged-insects from the water surface.

Dippers' inaccessible nesting sites, ability to swim under water, solitary habits, and their tendency to remain motionless on a rock above the surface of the water when danger approaches keep them safe from predators.

In addition to its strong wings and legs, it has a third eyelid called the "nictitating membrane" which protects the eyes from rushing water while still allowing clear vision. An oversize oil gland assures excellent waterproofing, and small flaps over the nostrils keep water out. Its all- gray body, short tail, dipping motion, and habitat make it easy to identify. It is the only bird in its family in the U.S. so it is one of a kind. Found along western mountain streams, it can be seen in the upper park above the Five Mile recreation area, both the winter and summer.

Rarely venturing very far from its home stream, the American Dipper nests alongside the rushing water as well, building a roundish nest nearby, often entirely of moss, even behind a waterfall.

Ruby-crowned Kinglet
UPPER & LOWER PARK

The Ruby-crowned Kinglet is fairly common all through the forested areas of the park in the winter and early spring, this grayish green bird occasionally displays its ruby-red crest, the source of its name, meaning "little king". Although the female does not have a crest, both sexes have a white eye ring and a lower wingbar bolder than the upper. One of the smallest of songbirds at a bit over four inches, it would be inconspicuous were it not for its flighty behavior, hopping frantically from branch to branch, wings flapping, seeking insects and spiders, their eggs and larvae. It often hovers over the tips of branches, swooping down to pick up its prey. It occasionally eats berries, tree sap, and even nectar as well.

Migratory throughout most of the U.S. they are permanent residents of California. Easy to spot in the winter when the leaves are gone and the birds are actively feeding, they become more wary and inconspicuous when breeding season begins. They build a small nest of bark, moss, grass, lichens, twigs, pine needles, and line the outer walls with spider webs. The inside of the nest is lined with feathers and fuzzy plant parts. It may be a hanging nest or a cup nest on a branch or a hybrid (semi-hanging) construction. Laying up to a dozen eggs, the Ruby-crowned Kinglet has the greatest egg to body weight ratio of any songbird; the total weight of the eggs may exceed that of the female that laid them!

Very similar in appearance and behavior to the kinglet, the resident Hutton's Vireo has a wider bill, an incomplete eyering, equally bold wingbars and no crest.

The Ruby-crowned Kinglet population is increasing across the country. Most likely, its adaptability to a variety of forested habitats and wide range of food items accounts for its success. Look for these little gems especially on the CSU campus and in Lower Park in the winter, although they are nearly everywhere there are trees and shrubs.

Blue-gray Gnatcatcher
UPPER & LOWER PARK

The rather silly name of the Blue-gray Gnatcatcher refers to its insectivorous habits, but eating very small gnats would not be very productive. A small bird with a long tail and wide eye ring, and white outer tail feathers, it somewhat resembles the Ruby-crowned Kinglet, which has a shorter tail and less distinctive eye ring. The gnatcatcher tail may make up almost half its total length and is often flipped up and down or held vertically while the bird is foraging. It almost looks like a small Northern Mockingbird. Males and females look very similar. They are fairly rare in the park as parasitism by Brown-headed Cowbirds has severely reduced their population.

In addition to looking like a small mockingbird, the Blue-gray Gnatcatcher incorporates songs of other species into its songs as well.

Blue-gray Gnatcatchers inhabit a wide variety of wooded habitats throughout the park in the summer, where they actively glean insects off foliage. They will also flush their prey off of branches and leaves, then hover and sally to catch them. Blue-gray Gnatcatchers feed mostly near the tips of branches in broad-leaved trees and large shrubs. Gnatcatchers search for food by moving up and down through the outer foliage and sometimes along branches toward the trunk, peering with quick head movements. They flick their white-edged tail from side to side, trying to scare up insects.

The nest is an open cup made from plant material, spider web, and flakes of lichen, attached to a horizontal branch. Males help out with nest construction, incubation and feeding of young. Four or five pale blue eggs with brown spots hatch in about two weeks. Fledging occurs 10-12 days later. Both parents bring food to the young. Although both the male and female contribute to the care of the eggs and hatchlings, they do not interact with one another after incubation begins. They often fledge a second brood together later in the season.

The calls and songs are very high in pitch and often hard to detect.

Western Bluebird
UPPER & LOWER PARK

One of the most recognizable of all birds, the Western Bluebird signals renewal and the arrival of spring and has become a significant icon of happiness and joy in American culture. There are bluebirds in Bidwell Park throughout the year; residents are joined by some winter bluebird visitors from farther north. Fairly drab in the winter and fall with a grayish back and light tan front, the male bursts into breeding season with a bright blue back and bright orange breast with a bluish belly beneath; the female is much duller.

Western Bluebirds are found in open forests, grasslands and agricultural areas. They are frequently seen perching on a fence wire or post or a tree branch from which they sally out to catch insects on the ground and occasionally in midair; in the winter they will eat berries.

Being cavity nesters, the male seeks a dead snag, fence post or birdhouse to center his territory around and attract a female. After mating, the female does most of the nest building and it is not uncommon to discover that the male is mating with another female while this construction occurs. After the eggs hatch, Tree Swallows have been known to help feed the young bluebirds and then use the same nest box later. The felling of dead trees, the disappearance of wooden fence posts, and the usurping of nesting holes by House Sparrows and European Starlings has led to a decline in Western Bluebirds.

Up to 45% of young bluebirds in a nest are not fathered by the male of the pair that built the nest.

They are naturally aggressive at nesting time and attack intruders fiercely. Western Bluebirds frequently set up housekeeping near human habitation. Often a male bluebird will actively attack his own reflection in a house window, an automobile windshield or side-view mirror, or any other metal or glass that provides a reflection.

American Robin
UPPER & LOWER PARK

The American Robin is perhaps the most familiar of all birds in the U.S. and although it has the reputation of being the first indication of spring, it is resident over almost all of the U.S. in summer and winter and can be found almost anywhere in Bidwell Park any time of year. The male's robin-red breast is distinctive; the female is a bit duller, and immature birds have a spotted breast. Most robins that breed in far northern North America migrate south, so robins are more abundant in winter than summer in the park. About ten inches in length, robins can be seen mainly in woodlands, gardens, orchards, lawns, and fields, preferring open ground for foraging, with a few scattered trees and shrubs for nesting and roosting. Suburban, park and agricultural areas provide these habitats, so American Robins are common near human habitation. This bird forages on a wide variety of fruits and berries, worms, grubs and caterpillars. In summer it is often seen on lawns in the morning looking for earthworms; in winter, its diet is made up largely of berries.

Robins often ingest lead left over from leaded gasoline and paint; contaminated soil particles adhere to the skin of worms which the birds pull from lawns.

In the winter they may forage in large flocks. When spring arrives the flocks break up and individuals form pairs, the male singing his familiar song. The female builds a cup-shaped nest of twigs held together with a bit of mud; she then lays and incubates three to five "robin's-egg blue" eggs.

The American Robin is a thrush and its very appropriate scientific name, *Turdus migratorius*, means "wandering thrush." Unlike many bird species, populations of American Robins are increasing, most likely due to the conversion of wild habitats to suburbs and the decreasing use of pesticides.

Hermit Thrush
UPPER & LOWER PARK

The Hermit Thrush is a migrant over most of North America and is a common winter resident of Bidwell Park. Smaller than the similarly-shaped robin, this brownish thrush has a distinctive rufous-colored tail, a white eye-ring and a spotted breast. Its name comes from its supposed shyness, although it is often seen in the open.

Thrushes inhabit forests and forest edges, often feeding on the ground. Most species are gray or brown in color, often with speckled underparts. Thrushes prefer insects, but most species will also eat worms, snails, and fruit. Hermit Thrushes do much of their foraging on the ground, hopping along, picking food up from the leaf litter or soil. Thrushes build cup-shaped nests, sometimes lining them with mud in which they lay two to five speckled eggs. The Hermit Thrush is one of the most widely distributed forest-nesting, migratory birds in North America, nesting in coniferous and mixed woodlands. Both parents help in raising the young. Hermit Thrush males winter farther north than do females, allowing them to set up territories in the spring before the females arrive.

The word "thrush" comes from the Welsh for starling; in olde English it also means a "lazy person."

The songs of some thrush species are considered to be among the most beautiful of bird songs. The Hermit Thrush's song is ethereal and flute-like, often sung from a high open location. Because it is soft and emanates from deep in the woods, the hermit's song is often overlooked. A Native American legend has it that birds had no song at one time and a bird would have to rise high into the spirit world to get one. The Hermit Thrush could not fly that high, so it hitched a ride in the feathers of an eagle. It was given the song but was so embarrassed it cheated it now stays hidden on the forest floor.

Northern Mockingbird
UPPER & LOWER PARK

The Northern Mockingbird is perhaps best known for singing all night. Songbirds begin to sing in response to the amount of daylight and the sequential singing of songbirds in the morning is known as the "Dawn Chorus". On overcast days, the chorus starts later. Mockingbirds are stimulated to sing by a small amount of light, even moonlight, and can imitate a large variety of songs of other birds as well as those of insects, although it is arguable how accurate these imitations are. Only the unmated males sing all night; males with a mate sing only during the day. An individual Mockingbird may have a repertoire of up to 200 songs and tends to repeat each of them twice.

The scientific name of the mockingbird, Mimus polyglottos, means "mimic of many tongues".

In the 18th and 19th centuries in the eastern U.S., Mockingbirds were in demand as caged birds because of their singing skills, leading to their near decimation. Populations have rebounded and expanded and they now are found from Canada to mid-Mexico, but are much more common in the middle of the U.S. and southward. Their ranges move north and south with the climate, warming climate allowing them to move farther north. The spread of suburbia has provided more habitat for them as well. They were not commonly seen in Chico until about 1980 and appear to be increasing in number.

Mostly gray in color, their Robin-size body of about ten inches, long downcurved bill, long black tail with white outer tail feathers, and obvious large white patches in their wings make them easy to identify, especially in flight.

During breeding season male birds become very demonstrative, raising their wings and flashing their white wing patches. Mockingbird pairs defend their territory and will dive at dogs, cats and humans during the breeding season. They build their nests in thick brush and feed exclusively on berries and invertebrates.

They can recognize threatening figures such as humans or cats that have approached their nest on a previous occasion and will attack them.

European Starling
UPPER & LOWER PARK

The European Starling is a non-native species that has become naturalized since its introduction in 1890 into New York's Central Park by a group of people who wanted to introduce all the birds in Shakespeare's plays into the U.S. By the 1940's they had reached California and started nesting in Chico about 1947. Today they are found from Alaska to northern Mexico. As an introduced species, they are not protected by the Migratory Bird Act. A very adaptable species, the starling has readily acclimated to urban and rural habitats. Nesting in cavities which they are unable to create for themselves, they displace other bird species such as nuthatches and woodpeckers by driving them from their nesting holes.

It is easy to distinguish a Starling in flight as a silhouette with a short tail and the wing shaped like a right triangle, with the rear edge of the wing as the hypotenuse, easily seen in flight.

Although not considered very attractive birds, a closer look reveals iridescent greenish-black plumage during the breeding season. In the winter the European Starling has white tips on its body feathers in fresh plumage, giving a spotted appearance in fall and winter. These tips wear off, leaving the purple-green iridescent black plumage of the breeding season; this is known as "wear plumage." In addition, the black bill sported in the winter is wiped on branches and by the time spring arrives, the pigment will have worn off and a bright yellow bill will have appeared.

Starlings, relatives of Mynah birds, exhibit varied songs, with warbling and gurgling sounds and are good mimics, imitating other birds such as the Killdeer and Western Meadowlark as well as car alarms, sirens, and telephones. Starlings are found mainly in human created environments, such as farms, suburbs, cities, and mown fields. They can be seen almost anywhere in Bidwell Park, especially the lower park. Starlings eat a variety of food such as insects and worms, fruits and berries, grain, cattle feed and even garbage. Year-round, European Starlings roost together at night, even during breeding season, often in large numbers.

Cedar Waxwing
UPPER & LOWER PARK

Cedar Waxwings are found in groups feeding on berries throughout the park in the winter. They get their name from the red tips of some of their wing feathers which appear to have been dipped in sealing wax. (A document that was so sealed was a legitimate document and the seal became equivalent of a legal signature today.) But the number of red tips varies from zero to ten on individual birds. The ends of the tail feathers are yellow, the color coming from the plant material the birds ate. If they happen to have eaten certain red berries while their tail feathers were forming, the tips might be red or orange. Also characteristic are the smooth, silky plumage, the noticeable topknot, and a black mask outlined in white. Topknots are great features to tell bird species apart. The only other bird that looks anything like a Cedar Waxwing is the larger Bohemian Waxwing which is extremely rare in Bidwell Park and might only be seen during exceptionally cold winters. In addition, the Cedar Waxwing is six to seven inches in length while the Bohemian Waxwing is seven to eight inches long and more rotund. The Oak Titmouse has a topknot but is a bit smaller and is an evenly dull gray color.

Occasionally a cedar waxwing will become incapacitated or even die from eating berries that have fermented.

The food of the waxwing consists primarily of fleshy fruit but they will take insects. They have an efficient digestive system which can separate the fruit from the seed and the seed defecated in about 16 minutes! Gregarious birds, they sometimes pass a berry from bird to bird until one decides to eat it. They are usually seen in flocks of ten to 50 birds. Sitting together on a branch or wire, individuals will sometimes pass berries around to each other.

They do not have a song but several calls which can only be described as thin whistles or buzzes. Look for them throughout the park primarily in the winter, but they are possible almost any time of the year.

Yellow Warbler
UPPER & LOWER PARK

The Yellow Warbler breeds over almost all of North America and winters in Central and South America. Sometimes called "yellow bird" or "wild canary", this five-inch bird is the most widespread of all warblers. Yellow Warblers are bright yellow birds with upperparts having a slight greenish tinge, and greenish yellow tails. Their heads and faces are plain. Males have reddish streaks down their breasts and bellies. Females are less bright and have no reddish streaks.

Although similar in some ways to the goldfinch, this bird lacks the black wings and tail and has a smaller and more tapered bill. Its cheerful, bright call, described as *sweet, sweet, I'm so sweet* can be heard from willows, small trees, and shrubs growing on wet grounds and in residential areas with small ornamental trees.

Its diet is mainly insects and it seems to prefer juicy caterpillars, but will occasionally eat fruits and berries. Like most warblers, it uses a variety of foraging methods, including flying out to capture flying insects, climbing through vegetation and gleaning insects from vegetation foliage, or hovering and gleaning insects.

Unlike some other warbler species, its numbers are stable as it is able to adapt to forest edges and disturbed forest areas. A few Yellow Warblers nest in Bidwell Park, usually near water, but more are here in the winter. Like many songbirds, Yellow Warblers build a cup-shaped nest built of moss, grasses, lichen and even fur five to fifteen feet high in trees or bushes. Often parasitized by Brown-headed Cowbirds, this warbler may build a second nest on top of the first, completely covering the cowbird's eggs, and any of its own in the bottom layer. Nests with up to six layers have been found.

> *Although the annual mortality rate of Yellow Warblers has been determined to be 50%, some have survived to the age of ten in the wild.*

Wilson's Warbler
UPPER & LOWER PARK

The Wilson's Warbler is a small, less than five inches, active warbler found in brush and woodland edges, usually foraging on insects low in the vegetation. They can be distinguished by a greenish back, yellow undersides and a black cap although the cap may be indistinguishable in the female. They flick their wings and tails like kinglets. Not particularly wary of humans, you will most likely see them during spring migration in both Lower and Upper Park near the creek in low brush.

Alexander Wilson, considered by some to be the father of American ornithology, was a 19th century ornithologist and artist who decided to publish a book illustrating all the birds of North America, resulting in the nine-volume *American Ornithology* (1808-1814), illustrating 268 species of birds, 26 of which had not been previously known. In 1810, a meeting with J.J. Audubon, who noted the success of Wilson's works, likely encouraged the younger man to pursue bird painting as well. The Wilson's Warbler, as well as a phalarope, plover, and storm-petrel were named after him.

Wilson's Warblers migrate to their wintering grounds in Central America at night, sometimes alone, sometimes in groups, often with several species.

The Wilson's Warbler's diet is typical of the warbler family, consisting mostly of small arthropods which it gleans off leaves and branches but also flycatches in midair; it will also eat berries. The main insect diet appears to consist of bees, beetles, and caterpillars. The Wilson's Warbler sometimes eats the liquid produced by scale insects which excrete tree sap that they pass through their digestive system.

Breeding bird surveys indicate that the Wilson's Warbler is in decline, as high as two percent per year. Likely causes are disappearance or disturbance of riparian habitat, nest parasitism by the Brown-headed Cowbird, recreational activities, pesticides, and predation by feral and domestic cats. Other predators are jays, hawks, and garter snakes.

Black-throated Gray Warbler
UPPER & LOWER PARK

The Black-throated Gray Warbler nests in shrubby pine and oak-pine forests mostly west of the Rocky Mountains and is a short-distance migrant, wintering in Mexico and southern California. But it does nest in the Upper Park where you may hear its cat-like calls from March to June.

The warblers feed mainly on insects, especially caterpillars, as they actively forage in low foliage and occasionally capture prey in flight. They build a typical open cup-shaped nest in which they lay three to five eggs which both parents incubate. The coloration and pattern of the bird's plumage camouflages it well but it will also feign a broken wing to distract predators should they approach the nest. Their call can be described as "*see see see , buzzeee*".

This bird's scientific name is Dendroica nigrescens, *which means "a bird of the woods in the process of becoming black".*

There are nearly fifty species of warblers that breed in North America but only about a dozen found commonly in California. Warblers, named for their melodious songs, play a very important role in the environment. They arrive on their breeding grounds at the same time trees are leafing out, which is also when may destructive insect pests emerge. Warblers generally feed on tree trunks and branches, gleaning insects, their larvae, and eggs. They occasionally will fly and capture insects in mid air, a technique called "hawking". Some classic studies have shown that different warbler species will divide a tree into zones, each species preferring a particular zone such as the top, the lower crown, or in the middle near the trunk. This reduces competition for food and is beneficial to all the individuals that feed on the tree.

Most male warblers are easy to identify because of their song and striking and colorful plumage, but in the fall, when males do not sing and don a plumage similar to that of females and immature birds, their identification can be a challenge.

Yellow-rumped Warbler
UPPER & LOWER PARK

The Yellow-rumped Warbler is common and abundant all through the park throughout the winter. Considerably duller than breeding plumage, its winter dress is still attractive and distinctive. Although the amount of yellow on the sides and head and the white on the throat varies, the yellow rump is always there, but can hidden or inconspicuous as it is in the illustration. Sometimes these birds are referred to as "butter butts".

Male Yellow-rumped Warblers forage higher in a tree or shrub than do females.

Warblers can be distinguished by their small size, slender bill, and flighty movements. They prefer insects, catching them on the ground or in foliage, or flying to capture them in mid-air. But they will also eat berries, especially in the winter. The warbler name, as you might imagine, comes from their complex and melodic songs.

The Yellow-rumped Warbler is migratory, and many spend the winter in the California Valley, but non-migratory populations can be found on the California coast where they both breed and winter. They are gregarious in winter and found in flocks of varying sizes. They are the last of the warblers to arrive and the last to leave because of their generalized requirements and willingness to inhabit human-influenced habitats.

Two million years ago or so, North America was divided into eastern and western zones by glaciers, separating this species into two forms which diverged in appearance and were at one time considered two species, the western Audubon's Warbler and the eastern Myrtle Warbler. Both were combined into one species, the Yellow-rumped Warbler as recent DNA evidence confirms that they are actually one species with some plumage variation. The eastern race can winter farther north than any other warbler because of its dependence on Myrtle berries; in fact, the birds' winter distribution is closely tied to the range of the Myrtle bushes.

Townsend's Warbler
UPPER & LOWER PARK

Townsend's Warblers are easy to identify as they have various contrasting patterns of color. Their backs are greenish and their wings are gray with two white wing bars. The heads of males have black and yellow stripes and the black face mask is punctuated by an elongated yellow spot under the eye. Their throats and breasts are yellow with black streaks on the sides. The females are similar, but duller. Where they occur together in northern California, Oregon, and Washington, Hermit and Townsend's Warblers hybridize. The less common Hermit Warbler is similar but has a yellow face bordered vertically by black cap and throat. Both species winter from the coast of northern California on down to Central America.

Townsend's Warblers breed in coniferous forests so they are only found in Bidwell Park during migration in spring and fall and occasionally during the winter. Like most warblers, their diet consists mostly of insects during the breeding season but in the winter is supplemented by berries. The male will begin to sing on its wintering grounds before migration, probably to perfect his song. After arrival on the breeding site the male establishes a territory and courts a female. The female then builds a nest in a coniferous tree but if the site turns out to be less than suitable, she moves all the materials of the nest to another nest site.

Nathaniel Wyeth, a wealthy ice harvester, led an expedition to Oregon in 1834, accompanied by John Kirk Townsend, a pharmacist and physician, and Thomas Nuttall, a botanist. Bird specimens taken by Townsend were an important contribution to Audubon's paintings. These included birds such as Vaux's Swift, Sage Thrasher, Black-throated Gray Warbler, and Townsend's Warbler.

Although Townsend first described this warbler, he used his name only because it was chosen by Thomas Nuttall, thus avoiding the unspoken rule of not naming a bird after oneself.

Orange-crowned Warbler
UPPER & LOWER PARK

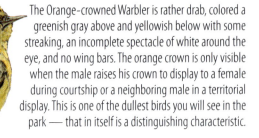

The Orange-crowned Warbler is rather drab, colored a greenish gray above and yellowish below with some streaking, an incomplete spectacle of white around the eye, and no wing bars. The orange crown is only visible when the male raises his crown to display to a female during courtship or a neighboring male in a territorial display. This is one of the dullest birds you will see in the park — that in itself is a distinguishing characteristic.

These birds prefer the lower vegetation levels and nest in Bidwell Park in the low brush or on the ground under oak trees or shrubs. This nesting behavior makes them very susceptible to predation by cats and other mammalian predators. In the fall they depart for more southern states and Central America, although a few might winter in the park. They breed, migrate through, or nest in all of North America, so they are a very common warbler, but probably the most misidentified. They can be confused with the Nashville Warbler which migrates through Bidwell Park in the fall, but the Nashville Warbler has a complete eye ring and brighter yellow belly. Like most warblers their summer diet is mostly insects. Orange-crowned Warblers will also feed on flower nectar, and occasionally visit hummingbird feeders and the sap wells drilled by sapsuckers.

The Orange-crowned Warbler's scientific name, **Vermivora celata,** *means the concealed worm eater.*

Most birds are infected by external parasites such as lice, mites, ticks or blowflies. In the Orange-crowned Warbler two species of lice have evolved a very close relationship to this bird. The mites only reproduce during the breeding season of the Orange-crowned Warbler. Lice feed on blood and their reproduction is stimulated by the rising level of reproductive hormones in the blood of the warbler. This ensures that new hosts, the young birds, are available to the next generations of lice.

Western Tanager
UPPER & LOWER PARK

The Western Tanager is unquestionably the most strikingly colorful bird one might spot in Bidwell Park. Wintering from very southern California nearly to South America, you will see it only on its migratory passage through the park in the spring and fall, although it is fairly sedentary and hard to spot. Tanagers as a group are mostly tropical, the Western Tanager being the most northerly, nesting as far north as the Northwest Territories in Canada and wintering from southern California to Costa Rica. The male is mostly yellow with a dark tail, two yellow wing-bars, and an orange-red head. The female is greenish-yellow above and yellow below. Both are about seven inches in length. You can find them almost anywhere in the forested areas of the park. In late spring and early summer, they feed primarily on insects, often flycatching from the tops of trees, but a small part of their diet later in the summer consists of fruits such as cherry, mulberry, elderberry and serviceberry.

On June 6, 1806, Capt. Lewis of the Lewis and Clark Expedition discovered the Western Tanager in Idaho.

The red head of the male is due to a red pigment that the bird has to ingest from insects which in turn have eaten fruits containing the red pigment. Because the birds eat varying amounts of different insects and the insect's diets vary as well, there is a good deal of variation in the amount of red on the head and the intensity of the color.

A good portion of this bird's southern habitat has been lost due to the destruction of its native wintering habitat in the tropics, but in some cases, coffee is being grown under a tall canopy of shade-giving trees which simulates the native habitat. Studies in Colombia and Mexico found 94-97% fewer bird species around sun-grown coffee than shade-grown coffee. So shade-grown coffee is beneficial to birds.

Recent evidence seems to indicate that North American tanagers are actually a part of the sparrow family.

Black-headed Grosbeak
UPPER & LOWER PARK

The medium-sized Black-headed Grosbeak is an aptly named bird with its heavy beak and the black head of the male contrasting with a rusty- orange underside, nape and rump and a black back with white patches. The much duller female has a light orange breast, brown head, and a long white stripe from the beak over the eye onto the nape. Arriving in late April from their wintering grounds in Mexico, they are usually first noticed by their song, which is very similar to an American Robin's, but smoother and faster. Typically they sing from a conspicuous perch high in a tree and can be found in all wooded areas of the park.

The Black-headed Grosbeak is one of the few bird species able to eat the Monarch Butterfly which contains toxic chemicals and protects the butterflies from most predators.

The Black-headed Grosbeak forages from the treetops to the forest floor on berries, nuts, and especially seeds but while nesting they eat more insects, spiders, worms, and other invertebrates, including large grasshoppers. They are most often found in mixed deciduous woodlands, especially in riparian areas, but also frequent bird feeders in suburban neighborhoods.

Like many songbirds, the male is brightly colored as he needs to attract females and defend his territory. The bright color and complex song are his advertisements. The female's duties are to lay eggs and raise the young as inconspicuously as possible so as not to attract competitors or predators, hence her duller plumage, although the pair share parental duties, the male being bright below and dull above, hiding his bright plumage while incubating. The female's call is similar to that of the male, prompting some ornithologists to believe that she is imitating another male in order to keep her mate around the nest. Their nest bottoms are often so thin they are almost transparent; apparently this flimsy construction helps in ventilating the nest in hot climates such as Chico.

Spotted Towhee
UPPER & LOWER PARK

The Spotted Towhee gets its name from the spots on the wing and back and the towhee from its call. Once called the Rufous-sided Towhee, the species has been split into the western Spotted Towhee and the Eastern Towhee. Typically seen as individuals, they can be heard scratching on the ground with both feet at once, uncovering invertebrates and seeds under leaves and twigs. Towhees are easy to distinguish as they do a two-footed backwards hop during foraging, eating mainly seeds, although in the breeding season they prefer arthropods. About the size of a robin, the male, with its red eye, rusty sides, black head and white belly, is unmistakable. The female color pattern is much the same except that where he is black, she is brownish and a bit duller.

Pipilio maculatus, the scientific name of the Spotted Towhee, means the "Spotted Chirper."

Spotted Towhees live and nest in thickets and at the edges of brushy woodlands, gardens and shrubby park areas. The male establishes a territory and waits for the female to choose him as a mate. At this time, singing is loud and frequent. After a mate is chosen, singing diminishes greatly as it would only serve to attract predators and only a simple *chewink* call is heard. During the breeding season both sexes collect materials and build a cuplike nest of grass, twigs, weeds, bark, and stems often at the bottom of a tree branch or twig near the ground. The female lays two to six greenish or cream-colored eggs spotted with brown which she incubates for 12 to 13 days while the male brings her food and protects the nest. The male towhee helps to feed the young until they are ready to leave the nest ten to twelve days after hatching. Two broods are typically raised each year. Spotted Towhees occasionally sun themselves, lying down on the grass with feathers spread.

California Towhee
UPPER & LOWER PARK

The California Towhee is a fairly nondescript bird. Both sexes are a dull brown overall color with rusty underneath the tail and buff or rust colored streaks at the throat. Around ten inches in length with a longish tail, it gives the appearance of a large dull colored sparrow. A permanent resident of the far west coast from southern Oregon to Baja California, it is common in northern California and can be seen all over Chico and Bidwell Park. It nests from chaparral vegetation into the lower mountain slopes. The California Towhee is not migratory, but it makes limited movements from higher to lower elevations in bad winter weather winter.

The California Towhee prefers shrubby areas and it is common around parks and gardens and homes. Its secretive habits combined with its nondescript appearance make it a subtle and not very noticed bird. Like all towhees, it hops and scratches on the ground with both feet at once, stirring up insects and finding seeds underneath the litter. California Towhees are most often seen as individuals rather than groups. When disturbed or frightened, the towhee will run like a mouse rather than fly.

Along with robins and bluebirds, Brown Towhees have a habit of attacking their reflection in car windows and mirrors, thinking their reflection is an intruding competitor.

When a male approaches a female in courtship, he will often spread his wings and crouch low to the ground. Both males and females will sun themselves in this wingspread posture, presumably to dry their feathers, ridding themselves of parasites. They nest in branches or shrubs near the ground.

The name "towhee" originally came from the "eastern towhee" in the late 18th-century, which was named for its call. There has been a lot of discussion about the relationships of towhees and today there are considered to be seven species. A group of towhees is called a "teapot".

Lark & Chipping Sparrow
UPPER & LOWER PARK

The Lark Sparrow (right) and Chipping Sparrow (below) are not often seen but are both possible sightings, mostly in Upper Park but they can sometimes be found in the Lower Park as well. The Chipping Sparrow breeds in the park and is rare in winter while the Lark Sparrow only winters there. Both have a brown back and gray front with a rusty cap and a black line through the eye but the Chipping Sparrow has a solid rusty cap and a plain face while the Lark Sparrow has a black, white, and rusty patterned face and a spot in the center of its breast. The longer tail of the Lark Sparrow has conspicuous white triangles at its end.

Lark Sparrow

Chipping Sparrow

Both birds inhabit open areas adjacent to woodlands and feed on the ground. The Lark Sparrow is common around the Five Mile area ball fields. Like all sparrows their main diet is seeds and grain but during breeding season insects, especially grasshoppers, make up a much larger part of their diet because insects have about twice as much protein than seeds and young birds need that protein to grow. The Lark Sparrow nests on the ground while the Chipping Sparrow prefers to nest in a tree within 15 feet of the ground. The Chipping Sparrow is named after its chip call; its song is a trill. The Lark Sparrow is so named because its melodious call is reminiscent of a lark.

The Lark Sparrow walks while the Chipping Sparrow hops. The scientific name of the Lark Sparrow, **Chondestes grammacus,** *means "grain eater with striped head" while the Chipping Sparrow's name,* **Spizella passerina,** *means "ground finch".*

In the 1850's, the Chipping Sparrow was the most common city sparrow, displaced, no doubt, by the House Sparrow. Both Chipping and Lark Sparrows are declining in numbers due to the reduction of grassland habitat and parasitism by the ubiquitous Brown-headed Cowbird.

Golden-crowned Sparrow
UPPER & LOWER PARK

The Golden-crowned Sparrow has a yellow crown bordered by black; the immature birds have a brown streaked head with little or no yellow. Found only in the winter, they often accompany White-crowned Sparrows but are generally less abundant. They are seed-eaters but in the summer they will eat berries, shoots, flowers and buds and were considered a pest species early in the 20th century as they frequented vegetable gardens. Golden-crowned Sparrows are common at bird feeders in the winter where they establish a particular feeding site and always feed from that spot, even if no other birds are present. This way they become comfortable with the situation, not having to readjust every time they visit.

Alaskan gold miners called this bird Weary Willie, because of its call which to the miners sounded like "I'm so weary."

In the early spring they move northward from their wintering grounds on the U.S. west coast to their breeding grounds in Canada and Alaska where they nest in shrubby habitat above the treeline or near the coast. When breeding, Golden-crowned Sparrows, like many birds, pair up and build a solitary nest away from other birds. They build a nest on the ground in a natural depression so that the rim of the nest is a ground level.

Why do they become so sociable in the winter, flocking with not only their own kind, but one or more other species? There are two thoughts — it may simply be that more eyes and ears make watching for predators more efficient. The second is that food can not only be found more easily with more searchers, but as they feed together, there is little defense of the food supply and less aggression. The latter does not quite hold at a bird feeder because the food is concentrated in such a small space.

A group of Golden-crowned Sparrows is called a "reign" which seems appropriate for a bird with a crown.

White-crowned Sparrow
UPPER & LOWER PARK

The White-crowned Sparrow is easy to identify by its descriptive name. One of the first arrivals from the north in order to spend the winter in Bidwell Park, they are usually seen in flocks, among which are immature birds with a tan and brown-striped crown. Like all sparrows the plumage of the males and females are nearly identical. They can be seen almost everywhere in Bidwell Park on forest edges, shrubs, ball fields, the golf course, grasslands, backyards, and at feeders around Chico. They often associate in flocks with Golden-crowned Sparrows and Dark-eyed Juncos, all feeding on seeds, plant parts and invertebrates on the ground or low brush. Most White-crowned Sparrows are migratory, nesting in Canada and Alaska and wintering in the lower 48, but some are permanent residents of high elevation areas of the western states and the coast of California.

The White-crowned Sparrow's song is a complex and variable one, much studied by ornithologists. It begins with a few clear whistles and then breaks up into buzz-like notes. The song is variable but the voice so distinctive that some scientists can actually distinguish individual birds when they sing. Singing is infrequent in the winter and you will most often hear them make a *chink* call instead. Young birds are born with a genetic blueprint of their song but to create the complete characteristic song of the species, the young learn refinements from the adults the spring after hatching.

White-crowned Sparrows are monogamous, with the female initiating courtship, and nest on the ground. To avoid nest predation by squirrels, snakes, or birds, the parents fly back to the nest on the ground but stop several feet short of it, walking the final distance. When the adults return to their breeding grounds in the spring, they will nest very close to where they had nested the previous year.

> *Much of what is known about the physiology of migration has been discovered via observations and experimentation on White-crowned Sparrows.*

Song Sparrow
UPPER & LOWER PARK

Song Sparrows are brown above with darker streaks, white below with brown streaking and most, but not all, have a dark brown spot or patch in the middle of the breast. They have a brown cap, gray cheeks with a brown stripe through them and a long rounded tail. Permanent residents of the park, they are secretive when breeding but are often seen in groups in the winter, especially in wetter areas. They are one of the most common sparrows in the park in the winter after the Golden- and White-crowned. Although they are cryptically colored as they blend in with brown grasses and shrubs, their song is clear and easily heard and recognized by humans.

The Patuxent Bird Banding Lab notes that 616,651 Song Sparrows have been banded since 1955. Of these, 16,502 have been recaptured, a recovery rate of 2.67%.

Song Sparrows have a very melodious song, typically begun with two to three sharp notes followed by a series of trills and warbles. Each individual bird has a characteristic song which may have dozens of variations, so rarely is the song sung exactly the same more than a few times in a row. Bird songs are partly inherited and partly learned. Young birds learn by listening to adult birds during the breeding season after they were born. Adult birds learn to recognize the songs of neighboring birds, helping them to distinguish the territories of neighbors and females recognize their mate's song. Populations of Song Sparrows even have regional dialects or "accents". Partly because of their different dialects and partly because of their differences in coloration, there are at least 39 recognized subspecies of Song Sparrows in the United States, more than almost any other bird.

As Song Sparrows prefer brushy habitats, they have benefited from forest removal and their populations are holding steady, even with substantial Brown-headed Cowbird parasitism.

Dark-eyed Junco
UPPER & LOWER PARK

Once called the Slate-colored Junco, the Dark-eyed Junco looks a bit like a little executioner with a dark hood contrasting with a lighter back and white belly. The hood varies from light gray to black and the back and sides from brownish to gray. There are as many as three to twelve subspecies based on these plumage variations, but all have dark eyes, a pink bill, and white outer tail feathers. Seen most often in groups in the winter, their white outer tail feathers may help to keep the group together in flight, warn the flock when danger approaches as the white tail feathers appear when members of the group take off, and they may be a mechanism to fool predators as the white feathers disappear from view when the birds land.

The name "junco" may derive from the Spanish word meaning "rush", referring to a water-loving plant, but juncos prefer drier areas such as open woodlands and grasslands. Dark-eyed Juncos feed in flocks on grass and grain seeds during the winter, often mixing with sparrow species in open areas such as grasslands, lawns, and golf courses. The junco flock shows a distinct hierarchy or "pecking order", with dominant individuals protecting the best feeding sites in the area.

The Dark-eyed Junco is colloquially known as the "snowbird" because in some areas it arrives about the time of the first snowfall of the year.

When the juncos head north or to higher elevations in the spring to their breeding grounds in coniferous or mixed forests where they nest on the ground, the males leave first to establish territories for the females who arrive later. Juncos are permanent residents on the west coast and parts of northern California, so you might see them at other times of the year, but they are most common in the winter in Bidwell Park.

Western Meadowlark
UPPER PARK

The Western Meadowlark is easily distinguished by its ski sweater of bright yellow with a black V-neck, and when it flies low across the ground, you can see its white outer tail feathers. The back is brown streaked and the crown black. About eight inches tall, it is frequently seen and heard singing from the top of fence posts or rails during the breeding season.

One of the most melodious birds, its song is an easily identifiable series of flutelike notes descending in pitch. Found mainly in the upper park, it is a resident of grasslands where it probes in the grass and soil for insects and seeds with its long and pointed bill. In the summer, when raising young, insects are its primary food. In the winter when insects are scarce, seeds and waste grain comprise their primary diet and flocks of 20 or more meadowlarks can be seen feeding by themselves or with other species of blackbirds. You may see Western Meadowlarks perched in oak trees above Horseshoe Lake.

Meadowlarks have strong "gaping" muscles which allow them to push their bills into the ground and spread the grass roots and soil apart to probe for insects and seeds.

A male meadowlark will mate with one, two, or even three females in the spring after chasing them as part of the courtship display. After mating, the females construct a nest, concealing it in a slight depression in the ground, sometimes a cow hoofprint, and lining it with fine grass, building grass walls, and covering the woven grass nest with a dome and a side entrance leading to a tunnel which may be over a foot long. After the average five young hatch, the female cares for them but the male may help in feeding.

The bright yellow breast and melodious song of the Western Meadowlarks serve as mutual signals for courtship and for establishing and defending a territory of about seven acres. But to avoid predators, a meadowlark will crouch low in the grass, hiding its belly and exposing only the cryptically colored back.

Brown-headed Cowbird
UPPER & LOWER PARK

The Brown-headed Cowbird is well known for its life style as a nest parasite; that is, it lays its eggs in other birds' nests, allowing the host species to raise the cowbird's young. A female cowbird may lay over 50 eggs in a season this way. The young cowbirds grow rapidly and aggressively compete for food brought to the nest, starving the host's young. Occasionally the young cowbirds will eject their host nestmates. In nearly three-quarters of the parasitized nests, the cowbird removes a host egg before laying her own. This may be to ensure that the host does not notice a change in the number of eggs in the nest.

Although this parasitic behavior certainly impacts individual bird nests, there is no strong evidence that the cowbird is responsible for the decline of the hosts they parasitize, although that may be the case in species with small or limited populations. Cowbirds parasitize about 220 species, but only about 150 are duped into raising cowbird young.

Brown-headed Cowbirds are found throughout the U.S. and before the arrival of colonists, followed bison, feeding on the insects the herds stirred up. Some think that cowbirds became parasitic because while following the bison they had little time to nest. Today they follow cattle and sheep and feed on waste grain, although they commonly nest in areas without livestock. They prefer open or semi-open country and are often found with flocks of European Starlings, Red-winged Blackbirds and Brewer's Blackbirds. Similar in size, shape, and coloration to the Brewer's Blackbird, the cowbird male has a brown head, shorter tail, and blunter bill than the Brewers; the Brewer's male also has a yellow eye. The females are similar but again the shorter tail and blunter bill distinguish the cowbird.

Cowbird young hatch earlier than the host young, giving the parasite an advantage in competing for food with its young and smaller host siblings.

Red-winged Blackbird
UPPER PARK

The Red-winged Blackbird is sexually dimorphic; the male is all black with a red shoulder with a yellow margin, while the female is a nondescript dark brown with darker streaks. About three-quarters of the annual Red-winged Blackbird diet is seeds and grain but during the breeding season they also eat insects, especially dragonflies, mayflies, and caddis flies. Males and females congregate in separate-sex flocks in the winter and migrate to their breeding grounds that way. The males migrate first and set up colonial territories in marshes, defending against other nearby males. The females arrive later and choose a mate depending on the quality of the male's territory. The polygamous males with the best territories may mate with five or six females. The males are very aggressive and may attack crows, herons, and humans encroaching on their territories. The males perch above the female and arch their backs and spread their wings to impress the female during courtship. After mating, the males defend their territory, nest, and young while the females tend to the domestic duties of incubating the eggs and caring for the young although the male will help supply some of the food. The nests are built of vegetation in rushes, bulrushes, or cattails a foot or two above the water of the marsh. Females blend right into their habitat with their brown speckled coloring. You may see them at Horseshoe Lake or slow flowing areas of the creek.

The red shoulder is critical to the males' success. Experimental studies in which the red epaulet was painted over with black caused the males to lose their territory!

The song of the Red-winged Blackbird is one of the most recognizable of all common birds. It has been described as sounding like a drawn out *ooo-gurgle-eee*.

Red-winged Blackbirds have been killed to limit crop predation and nuisance impacts, but some evidence shows that their impacts on crops have been overestimated.

Brewer's Blackbird
UPPER & LOWER PARK

The scientific name of the Brewer's Blackbird is *Euryphagus cyanocephalus*, a wonderfully descriptive Latin name which describes "a blue headed bird that eats a wide variety of foods." Seemingly black, the glossy plumage of the male shows a striking violet and blue-green iridescence in bright light, contrasting with a bright yellow eye. The duller female has a brown head, chest, and eye. The birds are eight to ten inches long with a bill shorter than the head. Brewer's Blackbirds are most often seen in agricultural areas but are found in other open areas as well such as most of Bidwell Park, parking lots, and suburban and urban settings. The spread of agricultural and suburban areas has benefited the Brewer's Blackbird and their range has been expanding north and eastward across the U.S. They are common in the Chico area.

Brewer's Blackbirds form flocks in the winter, often with other species of blackbirds and may winter in mixed flocks with other blackbirds. They are found throughout California and do not migrate although some may move down from higher elevations in the winter. They typically forage on the ground, walking and eating insects, worms, berries, seeds, grain, snails, and crustaceans, sometimes traversing shallow puddles. They often follow farm machinery as it stirs up insects and other invertebrates.

During courtship, the male displays by fluffing out his feathers, vibrating the wings, and pointing both the bill and tail upward. Brewer's Blackbirds nest in pairs or in small colonies. They prefer trees, but may nest on the ground, in shrubs, or in tall grass. The pair incubates four to six eggs and may nest twice in one season. Their song, typical of the harsh and unmelodious songs of many blackbirds, is high and squeaky.

Audubon named the blackbird after Thomas Mayo Brewer, an amateur ornithologist of the 19th-century and a contributor to Audubon's writings who probably never saw this bird in the field. (He also invented mayonnaise.)

Bullock's Oriole
UPPER & LOWER PARK

The Bullock's Oriole is medium-sized and closely related to the very similar Baltimore Oriole; both were once considered as one species, the Northern Oriole, and the two species produce fertile hybrids. This colorful bird is named after William Bullock, an English naturalist who collected many natural history specimens from the U.S. and Mexico in the 18th and 19th centuries.

"Oriole" comes from the Latin and means "golden", referring to the bird's color.

Bullock's Orioles migrate in flocks to southern Mexico and Central and South America in the winter and appear in Chico as early as late March. In Bidwell Park, they will stay about four months where they tend to prefer the tops of trees where they feed on flowers, fruit, spiders, nectar, and insects. Orioles often eat fruit and can be attracted with orange halves placed on platform feeders, or nailed to a tree or post. They return to their wintering grounds around the first of September, flying at night while navigating by the stars.

During courtship, the male stretches out and bows to the duller-colored female with wings spread and slightly raised. They build nests that resemble tightly woven pouches on the end of a branch, about six inches deep. The nest is sturdily built and will often incorporate pieces of string or yarn. The clutch of four to six eggs, mottled with brown, is incubated by the female for about two weeks at which time the young leave the nest.

Many bird species are parasitized by the Brown-headed Cowbird which lays its eggs in other birds' nests and lets them raise the young cowbirds. The Bullock's Oriole is one of the few hosts that actually recognizes the cowbird eggs and heaves them out of the nest, or just punctures them. It may even puncture some of its own eggs in the process, but the general result is beneficial to the oriole.

Evening Grosbeak
UPPER & LOWER PARK

The Evening Grosbeak male is a brightly colored bird while the female is mostly a dull green with some white in the wings. But they both have heavy bills that give them their name. Their scientific name, *Coccothraustes vespertinus*, means "seed eater of the evening" which is how the early pioneers described them. But grosbeaks may be seen any time of the day, usually in flocks in the tops of trees, eating berries and seeds in the winter. Their bills are so heavy and jaw muscles so strong that they can crack open cherry and olive pits. They occasionally ingest gravel to help their gizzard grind the large seeds they eat. Grosbeaks will also break twigs off sugar maple trees and ingest the sap.

In their coniferous forest breeding areas in the far north and the mountains of the west, the Evening Grosbeak eats primarily insects. When the spruce budworm, a favorite summer food of the birds, undergoes a population explosion, the Evening Grosbeaks have more young, may nest more than once in a season, and may even become polygamous that season because of the increased food supply. They are known as an "irruptive" species because their populations may increase substantially in only a few years. Those years, it is common to see large flocks, sometimes over 100 birds, around Chico. They are common in Lower Bidwell Park, around town, and will come to bird feeders which provide them with sunflower seeds. They are true wanderers and will continually travel to find food sources.

Grosbeaks are very agile seed eaters, using their bill to crack open sunflower seeds and their large thick tongue to scoop the seeds out before discarding the shells.

Unlike most songbirds that have a breeding and winter plumage, the major color change the Evening Grosbeak undergoes is that of its beak. A pale yellow in the winter, the pigment wears off and in the spring the male sports a lime green beak.

House Finch
UPPER & LOWER PARK

The House Finch, native to the southwestern U.S., was introduced into the northeast in the 1940's. The species is now resident throughout most of the U.S. A sparrow-like bird about six inches long with a cone-shaped bill, both sexes are a dull brown but the male displays a red wash over much of its underparts, the pigment coming from the food it has eaten, primarily red berries. Both sexes have streaked flanks, distinguishing this species from the similar Cassin's (which is not seen in Bidwell Park) and Purple Finches, which are redder and have fewer streaks. They are frequent visitors to bird feeders. Their call is an easily recognizable one consisting of a long series of chirps and warbles, often ending in a buzz.

The introduction into the northeastern U.S. was by a pet shop owner who illegally kept House Finches and released them so he would not get caught.

House Finches are native to open and desert habitats, but have expanded their range. They are now accustomed to human habitations and often nest around homes in cavity like places, even in garages, sheds, porches, hanging plant baskets, gazebos and even nests abandoned by other birds are used.

During courtship the male and female touch bills while the female imitates the posture and behavior of a young bird. The female prefers the reddest males as the red pigment comes from their diet and the intensity of the redness reflects the ability of the male to find food sources. The female does all the work of nest-building, but the male feeds the female during incubation and helps to feed the four to six young after they hatch.

House Finches are well known for their susceptibility to conjunctivitis which was discovered during the winter of 1993-1994. Symptoms of the disease are scabby, swollen, runny, cloudy-looking, or glassy eyes. Other species of birds are rarely affected and no one knows why House Finches suffer the most. You can see these birds in various areas of the park as well as around the university campus and city of Chico.

American & Lesser Goldfinches
UPPER & LOWER PARK

American and Lesser Goldfinches can be seen all year round but are most obvious in winter when the leaves are gone. The American Goldfinch male is bright yellow in the summer breeding season and an olive color during the winter months, while the female sports a dull yellow-brown which is only slightly brighter during the summer. The males' bright plumage is clearly intended to attract a female. Both are about four to five inches long. Their bright yellow colors have led people to call them "wild canaries." They breed in southern Canada and the northern U.S. and winter in most of the U.S. and down to Mexico. Lesser Goldfinches are resident all year and are similar to American Goldfinches but with greenish backs and a larger black cap. Immatures and females of both species are similar.

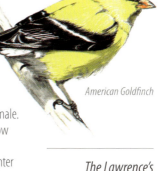

American Goldfinch

The Lawrence's Goldfinch breeds in the coastal and Sierra Nevada ranges and may be seen in the park on migration; their black faces distinguish them.

Lesser Goldfinch

During the breeding season they tend to be aggressive, defending territories against intruders. The American Goldfinch breeds later in the year than most finches and other birds, so they can take advantage of any plants that produce seeds later in the year. In the nest, made of plant fibers, the female lays four to six light blue eggs. The male feeds the female, who incubates the eggs for about two weeks.

Goldfinches are seed-eaters and have a conical beak and hard palate to grasp and crack seeds and agile feet to grip the stems of plants while feeding. Social birds, they gather in large flocks while feeding and migrating. Goldfinches are often seen in flocks of a dozen to several dozen birds, especially in the winter, foraging for seeds most often in open areas, such as grasslands. Human activity benefits the goldfinches as they are attracted to bird feeders, preferring small sunflower and niger seeds; they also eat the seeds of many ornamental trees such as crepe myrtle and weeds such as star thistle. Their flight call sounds like *po-ta-to-chip* while that of the American Goldfinch sounds like *per-chic-o-ree*.

House Sparrow
UPPER & LOWER PARK

The House Sparrow, once known as the English Sparrow, is probably the most widespread of all birds, having been introduced purposefully or accidentally to most areas of the world from its native European home. There probably is not a city or suburb in the world that does not have House Sparrows, or at least their very close and similar relatives.

In cold areas, House Sparrows will often roost in street lamps or other lights to stay warm.

In Chico you can find them almost anywhere and in Bidwell Park they are most common around playgrounds, open areas, ball fields, and poolsides, often living on the scraps of food humans discard.

Although often disdained for their scavenging habits, the males are rather attractive birds, especially compared to the very plain and dull female. There is no other species these five and a half inch birds can easily be confused with. Their unmelodious *chirp, chirp* is also well-known and distinctive.

In 1852, when many Europeans were immigrating to the U.S., House Sparrows were imported to bring a part of the "old country" to America, starting in Central Park. After a few unsuccessful introductions, House Sparrows took hold and now are found almost everywhere in North America and are probably the most abundant bird in the urban U.S. They will eat almost anything but prefer seeds, and nest almost anywhere. They have become a pest in some areas and, in a number of places, have displaced native birds. They are most successful in human-influenced habitats, though, and are not too much of a threat to birds that live in relatively undisturbed or harsh environments such as extensive forests.

The Migratory Bird act states that no birds or their parts or nests or eggs may be taken without a federal permit or appropriate hunting license. The House Sparrow, along with the European Starling and Rock Pigeon, is one of the few species of birds not protected by this federal law.

Other Birds You Might See

There are a number of other birds that are possible, but less likely, sightings, in Bidwell Park, than the birds noted in the book — but it happens. So here is a list of those birds, in the order you will find them in a typical bird field guide.

Great Egret

Bald Eagle, Golden Eagle

Ring-necked Pheasant

Black Rail. Sandhill Crane

European Collared Dove

Short-eared Owl, Spotted Owl, Northern Saw-whet Owl

Rufous, Black-chinned, Allen's Hummingbird, and more rarely, Costa's and Calliope Hummingbirds

Downy Woodpecker, Hairy Woodpecker, Lewis' Woodpecker, Williamson's Sapsucker

Dusky, Pacific Slope, Willow, Dusky, Gray and Hammond's Flycatchers Say's Phoebe, Western Wood Pewee

Hutton's vireo; common but often confused with very similar Ruby-crowned Kinglet

Steller's Jay, during cold winters

Northern Rough-Winged Swallow

Rock Wren, Canyon Wren, Marsh Wren

Varied Thrush, Mountain Bluebird, Townsend's Solitaire, in cold winters

California Thrasher

American Pipit

Wrentit

Phainopepla; fairly common behind the baseball diamonds and along the levee at the Hooker Oak area in the summer

Yellow-breasted Chat, Nashville Warbler, Hermit Warbler, MacGillivray's Warbler, Common Yellowthroat

Blue Grosbeak

Lazuli Bunting

Savannah Sparrow, Lincoln's Sparrow, Rufous-crowned Sparrow, Fox Sparrow

Purple Finch

Index

Acorn Woodpecker	28	Chipping Sparrow	65
American Goldfinch	77	Cliff Swallow	39
American Coot	16	Common Nighthawk	24
American Crow	38	Cooper's Hawk	9
American Dipper	46	Dark-eyed Junco	69
American Kestrel	12	European Starling	53
American Robin	50	Evening Grosbeak	75
Anna's Hummingbird	26	Golden-crowned Sparrow	66
Ash-throated Flycatcher	33	Great Blue Heron	1
Band-tailed Pigeon	19	Great Horned Owl	22
Barn Swallow	39	Green Heron	2
Barn Owl	21	Hermit Thrush	51
Belted Kingfisher	27	Herring Gull	15
Bewick's Wren	45	House Finch	76
Black Phoebe	32	House Sparrow	78
Black-headed Grosbeak	62	House Wren	45
Black-throated Gray Warbler	57	Killdeer	17
Blue-gray Gnatcatcher	48	Lark Sparrow	65
Brewer's Blackbird	73	Lesser Goldfinch	77
Brown Creeper	44	Loggerhead Shrike	35
Brown-headed Cowbird	71	Mallard	5
Bullock's Oriole	74	Mourning Dove	20
Bushtit	42	Northern Flicker	30
California Gull	15	Northern Mockingbird	52
California Quail	13	Nuttall's Woodpecker	29
California Towhee	64	Oak Titmouse	41
Canada Goose	3	Orange-crowned Warbler	60
Cedar Waxwing	54	Osprey	8

Red-breasted Sapsucker	31	Western Bluebird	49
Red-shouldered Hawk	0	Western Kingbird	34
Red-tailed Hawk	11	Western Meadowlark	70
Red-winged Blackbird	72	Western Screech Owl	23
Ring-billed Gull	15	Western Scrub Jay	36
Rock Pigeon	18	Western Tanager	61
Ruby-crowned Kinglet	47	White-breasted Nuthatch	43
Sharp-shinned Hawk	9	White-crowned Sparrow	67
Song Sparrow	68	White-tailed Kite	7
Spotted Towhee	63	Wild Turkey	14
Townsend's Warbler	59	Wilson's Warbler	56
Tree Swallow	40	Wood Duck	4
Turkey Vulture	6	Yellow Warbler	55
Vaux's Swift	25	Yellow-billed Magpie	37
Violet-green Swallow	40	Yellow-rumped Warbler	58

Bidwell Park
Chico, California

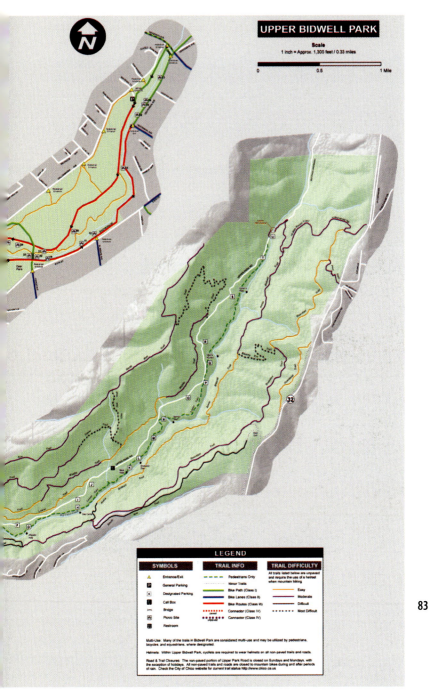

The Birds of Bidwell Park

Notes